On Travel and the Journey through Life

ON
TRAVEL
and the
JOURNEY
THROUGH
LIFE

EDITED BY
BARNABY ROGERSON
&
ILLUSTRATED BY
KATE BOXER

ELAND
London

First published by Eland Publishing Ltd
61 Exmouth Market, London EC1R 4QL in 2022

© Eland Publishing Ltd

ISBN 978 1 78060 204 2

Cover Images: *Dorothy Parker*, *James Baldwin*,
Tennessee Williams, *James Joyce* and *Dervla Murphy*
© Kate Boxer

Text set in Great Britain by James Morris
Printed in England by Clays Ltd, Elcograf S.p.A.

Contents

Preface

For forty years (1982–2022) Eland has been publishing travel books, driven by a fascination with human society in all its forms and a desire to celebrate those differences. There's an exhilarating variety of alternative ways of being, of different ways to think about the world around us and our position in it. And although we can't all take off for years to settle in a foreign land, learn the language, embed ourselves in a community and observe its complex relationships, we do all know about the liberation of leaving home.

Once far enough from our own hearth, we begin to see the ways that the walls around us have ossified our choices. Liberated from the tyranny of our schedules, we see that our time could be used more creatively, that we could inject greater variety into the rhythm of our lives. Immersing ourselves in the smells, tastes, sights and interests of another culture, we recognise the elements lacking in our own. Other people, *otherness*, is crucial to our understanding of ourselves. There is more than one right way to be, more than one perspective from which to think. And returning from our journey, there is space in which to continue to question our choices. But it's hard work to keep that space open and we need constant reminders of its importance.

This little book is designed to do just that. Dipping into it, you will find thoughts from our earliest recorded history and from yesterday, from European writers and from aboriginal peoples. Many are exhortations to live consciously. Echoing through the book is a *carpe diem*, a call to pay attention to the details of the journey rather than focussing on the destination. And throughout we are reminded of what Jonathan Raban calls 'the most ancient of all metaphors' – that life's a journey, from that first voyage down the birth canal to the last in a coffin.

Wandering through its pages, we hope you will find plenty which resonates with what matters to you at the moment.

Rose Baring
London, 2022

Acknowledgements

There are three people without whom this book would never have seen the light of day. Above all, we would like to thank our publicist Steph Allen for her work in gathering tips from travellers and epigrams on travel for our monthly Eland newsletter, which set Barnaby off foraging for more wisdom from around the globe. We would also like to thank Basil Bowdler, who did heroic work shaping this amorphous collection of material and Charlie Forrest, who put together the biographical sketches of the contributors.

The artist Kate Boxer kindly agreed to let us use her playful and loving portraits of writers who have inspired her. We are so delighted. If you would like to buy a print of any of them, please visit kateboxer.co.uk.

*I love quotations because it is a joy to
find thoughts one might have,
beautifully expressed with much authority by
someone recognised as wiser than oneself.*

Marlene Dietrich

ONE

A Single Step

> **A journey of a thousand miles
> starts with a single step.**
> *Lao Tzu*

> The world is a book and if you do not travel
> you read only one page.
> *St Augustine*

> Travel, in the younger sort, is a part of education;
> in the elder, a part of experience.
> *Francis Bacon*

> Certainly, travel is more than the seeing of sights; it is a change
> that goes on, deep and permanent, in the ideas of living.
> *Mary Ritter Beard*

That day, I really believed that I had grasped something and that henceforth my life would be changed. But insights cannot be held for ever. Like water, the world ripples across you and for a while you take on its colours. Then it recedes, and leaves you face to face with the void you must carry inside yourself, confronting that central inadequacy of soul

which you must learn to rub shoulders with and to combat,
and which, paradoxically may be our surest impetus.

Nicolas Bouvier

Three things cannot be long hidden;
the sun, the moon and the truth.

Buddha

The purpose of travel is to discover what ideas –
if those of the West are inadequate – can with greater
advantage guide our world.
Robert Byron

There is something pagan in me that I cannot shake off.
In short, I deny nothing, but doubt everything.

Lord Byron

Going up that river was like travelling back to the
earliest beginnings of the world, when vegetation
rioted on the earth and the big trees were kings.
Joseph Conrad

Travel has a way of stretching the mind. The stretch comes
not from travel's immediate rewards, the inevitable myriad
new sights, smells and sounds, but with experiencing first-
hand how others do differently what we believed to be the
right and only way.

Ralph Crawshaw

I know nothing, except my ignorance.
Diogenes

Too often travel, instead of broadening the mind,
merely lengthens the conversation.
Elizabeth Drew

I have no special talents.
I am only passionately curious.
Albert Einstein

To make a traveller an agreeable companion, it is necessary
not only that he should have seen much, but that he should
have overlooked much of what he has seen.

Henry Fielding

Two roads diverged in a wood, and I –
I took the one less travelled by,
And that has made all the difference.
Robert Frost

Better far off to leave half the ruins and nine-tenths of the
churches unseen and to see well the rest; to see them not
once, but again and often again; to watch them, to learn them,
to live with them, to love them, till they have become a part of
life and life's recollections.

Augustus Hare

There are only two rules for a traveller: be cheerful
and interested in everything. Do not bother too much
about your insides.

Frank Tatchell

> Keep the company of those who seek the truth –
> run from those who have found it.
> *Václav Havel*

Much learning does not teach understanding.
Heraclitus

Perhaps the greatest danger of our global community is that the person in LA thinks he knows Cambodia because he's seen *The Killing Fields* on-screen, and the newcomer from Cambodia thinks he knows LA because he's seen *City of Angels* on video.

> *Pico Iyer*

We must go beyond textbooks, go out into the bypaths and untrodden depths of the wilderness and travel and explore and tell the world the glories of our journey.
John Hope Franklin

> The first condition of understanding a
> foreign country is to smell it.
> *Rudyard Kipling*

Thanks to the Interstate Highway System,
it is now possible to travel across the country
from coast to coast without seeing anything.
Charles Kuralt

I preferred reading the American landscape as we went along.
Every bump, rise, and stretch in it mystified my longing.
Jack Kerouac

Travel light: an extra T-shirt, an extra pair of pants, an extra pair of socks is all you really need, along with some soap, a toothbrush and a piece of cloth big enough to be used as a towel, sarong, scarf or turban.

Barnaby Rogerson

Let us open the book of books.
Let us live, see and travel.
Lamartine

Too often … I would hear men boast of the miles covered that day, rarely of what they had seen.
Louis L'Amour

**The wise man is not he who gives the answers;
he is the one who asks the right questions.**
Claude Lévi-Strauss

Travelling through the world produces a marvellous clarity in the judgement of men. We are all of us confined and enclosed within ourselves and see no farther than the end of our nose. This great world is a mirror where we must see ourselves in order to know ourselves. There are so many different tempers, so many different points of view, judgements, opinions, laws and customs to teach us to judge wisely on our own, and to teach our judgement to recognize its imperfection and natural weakness.

Montaigne

Don't tell me how educated you are,
tell me how much you have travelled.
The Prophet Muhammad

On my tenth birthday a bicycle and an atlas
coincided as presents and a few days later
I decided to cycle to India.
Dervla Murphy

In our leisure we reveal what kind of people we are.
Ovid

Once the travel bug bites there is no known antidote, and I
know that I shall be happily infected until the end of my life.
Michael Palin

He who wishes to explore nature must tread her
books with his feet. Writing is learned from letters,
but Nature from land to land.
Paracelsus

A little learning is a dangerous thing.
Drink deep or taste not the Pierian spring.
Alexander Pope

Imperious and yet forlorn, coming through the silence of the
trees, the echoes of a golden horn, calling to distances.
Saki

The real voyage of discovery consists not in seeking new landscapes but in having new eyes.

Marcel Proust

Curiosity is the one thing invincible in nature.
Freya Stark

Not until we are lost do we begin to find ourselves.
Henry David Thoreau

Travel is fatal to prejudice, bigotry, and narrow-mindedness, and many of our people need it sorely on these accounts. Broad, wholesome, charitable views of men and things cannot be acquired by vegetating in one little corner of the earth all one's lifetime.
Mark Twain

Twenty years from now you will be more disappointed by the things that you didn't do than by the ones you did do. So throw off the bowlines. Sail away from the safe harbor. Catch the trade winds in your sails. Explore. Dream. Discover.

Mark Twain

There is no escaping the world, and no escaping
the effort to understand it.
James Whitfield

Make voyages! Attempt
them… there's nothing else.
Tennesse Williams

The world is full of magic things, patiently waiting
for our senses to grow sharper.
W B Yeats

TWO

Meetings and Collisions

Perhaps travel cannot prevent bigotry, but by demonstrating
that all peoples cry, laugh, eat, worry, and die, it can introduce
the idea that if we try and understand each other, we may
even become friends.
Maya Angelou

I love men, not for what unites them, but for what divides them,
and I want to know most of all what gnaws at their hearts.
Apollinaire

**I met a lot of people in
Europe. I even encountered
myself.**
James Baldwin

Great things are done when men and mountains meet.
William Blake

No matter where you go, there you are.
Buckaroo Banzai

The great difference between voyages rests not with the ships, but with the people you meet on them.
Amelia E Barr

What strange phenomena we find in a great city, all we need do is stroll about with our eyes open. Life swarms with innocent monsters.
Charles Baudelaire

I have fallen a hopeless victim to the Turk, he is the most charming of mortals.
Gertrude Bell

Nobody can discover the world for somebody else. Only when we discover it for ourselves does it become common ground and a common bond and we cease to be alone.
Wendell Berry

The subject matter of the best travel books is the conflict between writer and place.
Paul Bowles

The tongue can conceal the truth but never the eyes.
Mikhail Bulgakov

**A journey is best measured in friends,
rather than miles.**
Tim Cahill

It is the poor who give alms to the poor.
Traditional Chinese saying

To get away from one's working environment is, in a sense, to get away from one's self; and this is often the chief advantage of travel and change.
Charles Cooley

We live as we dream – alone.
Joseph Conrad

There are three things that make life worth living: to be writing a tolerably good book, to be at a supper table for six and to be travelling south with someone you love.
Cyril Connolly

Talk to a man about himself and he will listen for hours.
Benjamin Disraeli

What I like to drink most is the wine of others.
Diogenes

I think the devil doesn't exist,
but man has created him, he
has created him in his own
image and likeness.
Fyodor Dostoyevsky

Let us absorb the cultures of nations
and dissolve into our judgement all their codes.
William Empson

Go a hundred miles to speak with one wise man,
five miles to see a fair town.
Lord Essex to Lord Rutland (recalled by Samuel Johnson)

If customs and manners were everywhere the same,
there would be no office so dull as a traveller.
Henry Fielding

Carry pictures of your family. They are a great way of
communicating your harmlessness, especially when
language is an issue. If you don't have family, take pictures
of the royal family. They are often a source of interest.
John Gimlette

Being entirely honest with oneself is a good exercise.
Sigmund Freud

It is only in adventure that some people succeed
in knowing themselves – in finding themselves.
André Gide

He travels fastest who travels alone, but he laughs less.
Jason Goodwin

I expect to pass through this world but once; any good thing
therefore that I can do, or any kindness that I can show to any
fellow creature, let me do it now; let me not defer or neglect
it, for I shall not pass this way again.
Etienne de Grellet

Never go on trips with anyone you do not love.
Ernest Hemingway

Tea is an indispensable gift. What other gift works for
Muslims, Hindus, Jews, Buddhists, Russians, English
and the Irish? Also remarkably democratic ... even
with the fortune of Bill Gates at your disposal, you will
have to hunt very hard to get tea better than the foil-
wrapped teabags you can buy at Fortnums. Keeps its
flavour after months of travel.

John Hatt

The content of your character is your choice.
Day by day, what you choose, what you think
and what you do is who you become.
Heraclitus

> The best mirror is an old friend.
> *George Herbert*

The difficulty is not so great to die for a friend
as to find a friend worth dying for.
Homer

We travel, initially, to lose ourselves; and we travel, next, to find ourselves. We travel to open our hearts and eyes and learn more about the world than our newspapers will accommodate. We travel to bring what little we can, in our ignorance and knowledge, to those parts of the globe whose riches are differently dispersed. And we travel, in essence, to become young fools again – to slow time down and get taken in, and fall in love once more.
Pico Iyer

Travel on your own or, if you're in a group, run away from it as often as possible and talk to the locals. As John Steinbeck put it in *Travels With Charley*, 'two or more people disturb the ecologic complex of an area'.
Michael Kerr

> Don't be offended if a camel spits on you. Which he will. Interpret it rather as a sign of affection. It's all part of the bonding process.
>
> *Justin Marozzi*

A transition from an author's book to his conversation, is too often like an entrance into a large city, after a distant prospect. Remotely, we see nothing but spires of temples and turrets of palaces, and imagine it the residence of splendour, grandeur and magnificence; but when we have passed the gates, we find it perplexed with narrow passages, disgraced with despicable cottages, embarrassed with obstructions and clouded with smoke.
Samuel Johnson

Sir, I look upon every day to be lost, in which I do not make a new acquaintance.
Samuel Johnson

The traveller with empty pockets
will sing in the thief's face.
Juvenal

I loved you, so I drew these tides of men into my hands
and wrote my will across the sky in stars.
T E Lawrence

**I am looking for the people who have always
been there and belong to the places they live.
The others I do not wish to see.**
Norman Lewis

It's daunting to find the language so foreign, so distant, but
also so thrilling. One is absolved of responsibility when the
language is incomprehensible.
Frances Mayes

I have spent most of my life studying the lives
of other faraway peoples, so that Americans
might better understand themselves.
Margaret Mead

He who does not travel does not know the value of men.
Moorish proverb

Some practitioners maintain that the essential purpose of
moving around the world is to put yourself in other people's
shoes, to experience life… as Frenchmen or Israelis or
Japanese experience it, eating what they eat, buying what they
buy, even trying to think as they do. Not me. Nothing is going
to make a shogun of me, least of all ten days at a Yokohama
motel, and scholars who have spent entire careers studying
the Basque mind still can't make head nor tail of it. Far better
in my opinion to regard the great world as a kind of show,
a tragicomedy, kindly put on for my fascination. Nobody is
offended by this approach. Most people love to be looked at.
Jan Morris

Leave behind all technical gadgets without exception – live in the day and engage with the people you meet. Don't depend on keeping up the contacts of your non-travelling life – if you want to be in contact with them then stay at home.

Dervla Murphy

No matter how far you travel, you can never get away from yourself. It's like your shadow. It follows you everywhere.
Haruki Murakami

We can only learn to love by loving.
Iris Murdoch

The most effective way to destroy people is to deny and obliterate their own understanding of their history.
George Orwell

> Learn a word or two of modern Greek, think of a nice sounding name, look it up on the map and go there. Take to the hills and thank heaven for the fine tall gentlemen you meet. Eat and drink with them; ask what they think of the ruins and their history: and in a week you will learn more about Greece than twenty people who have motored everywhere for a month.
>
> *John Pendlebury*

God is man helping man.
Pliny

Truth comes out in wine.
Pliny

Teach me to feel another's woe, to hide the fault I see, that mercy I to others show, that mercy show to me.
Alexander Pope

Be to their virtue very kind; be to their faults a little blind.
Matthew Prior

It takes two to quarrel, but only one to end it.
Matthew Prior

People travel to wonder at the height of the mountains, at the huge waves of the seas, at the long course of the rivers, at the vast compass of the ocean, at the circular motion of the stars, and yet they pass by themselves without wondering.
St Augustine

I'm sick of just liking people. I wish to God I could meet somebody I could respect.
J D Salinger

People are often frightened of Parisians, but an American in Paris will find no harsher critic than another American.
David Sedaris

All this hurrying from place to place won't bring you any relief, for you're traveling in the company of your own emotions, followed by your troubles all the way.
Seneca

And when you're alone, there's a very good chance you'll meet things that scare you right out of your pants.
Dr Seuss

There is an internationalist uniform of baseball cap and nylon track suit that looks entirely at home at airports and motorway service stations. But if you are travelling to find something particular, your dress could indicate that you too have some pride in your community. Wear something that shows you have an identity and belong to a place that has spirit. In Oman, if you wanted something from the government, like a postage stamp or your pension, the Sultan asked his people to respect the offices of state by wearing their national dress.

Barnaby Rogerson

> Don't be paranoid – much better to be open and full of trust for people. The ones who are paranoid always get mugged anyway.
>
> *Hugh Thomson*

Journeys end in lovers meeting.
William Shakespeare

> The whole point of travelling is to arrive alone, like a spectre, in a strange country at nightfall.
> *Paul Theroux*

I have found out that there ain't no surer way to find out whether you like people or hate them than to travel with them.
Mark Twain

> Good friends, good books and a sleepy conscience: this is the ideal life.
> *Mark Twain*

> Travel alone if you're writing, researching, on a quest, or doing something madcap. Anyone along with you will only get bored and crabby, whilst you'll lose that essential vulnerability, spontaneity and need to engage with local people, so everyone loses. But travelling with someone else can be fun, too; keep things exciting by taking turns to dictate a whole day's programme.
>
> *Jasper Winn*

> Choose your companions carefully and be sure to include one troublemaker, possibly primed to play the part, whose carping, complaints and repugnant behaviour will unite the rest of your party in detestation of him or her and make you appear a paragon of good nature and sense.
>
> *Antony Wynn*

A single conversation across the table with a wise man is better than ten years study among fools.
Henry Wadsworth Longfellow

I have learned that to be with those I like is enough.
Walt Whitman

Some cause happiness wherever they go;
others whenever they go.
Oscar Wilde

I have always depended on the kindness of strangers.
Tennessee Williams

THREE

The Pleasures of the Road

He left me with enough to live on in a modest way, but I have never been very keen on modesty.
Aunt Augusta, from Graham Greene's Travels with My Aunt

One should always be drunk… with wine, with poetry, or with virtue, as you chose. But get drunk.
Charles Baudelaire

Taking food with friends has a sacramental dimension for me. It is part of the love of life.
Sybille Bedford

Travelling provides occasions for shaking oneself up but not, as people believe, freedom. Indeed it involves a kind of reduction: deprived of one's usual setting, the customary routine stripped away like so much wrapping paper, the traveller finds himself reduced to more modest proportions – but also more open to curiosity, to intuition, to love at first sight.
Nicolas Bouvier

She had learned to live light because life itself could be heavy enough.
Jackson Burnett

Nothing can go very far wrong at a table as long as there is honest bread, butter, olive oil and a generous spirit.
Sybille Bedford

We were not poor, we had everything we could carry.
Bushmen from Kalahari

I haven't got any special religion this morning.
My God is the God of Walkers. If you walk hard enough,
you probably don't need any other god.
Bruce Chatwin

You were not formed to live the life of brutes,
but virtue to pursue and high knowledge.
Dante

Wandering re-establishes the original harmony
which once existed between man and the universe.
Anatole France

Give me the clear blue sky over my head, and the green turf
beneath my feet, a winding road before me, and a three
hours march to dinner – and then to thinking!
William Hazlitt

Always say yes to tea. It is much the safest way to drink
water, and to both give and accept hospitality.
Rose Baring

> Travel as cheaply as you dare, and for less than you can afford: but spend liberally when you need to.
>
> *Jason Goodwin*

When preparing to travel, lay out all your clothes and all your money. Then take half the clothes and twice the money.
Susan Heller

In an age of speed, I began to think, nothing could be more invigorating than going slow. In an age of distraction, nothing can feel more luxurious than paying attention. And in an age of constant movement, nothing is more urgent than sitting still.

Pico Iyer

Take no gold, silver or copper to fill your purse, no pack for the road, no second coat, no shoes, no stick; the worker earns his keep… If anyone will not receive you or listen to what you say, then as you leave that house or town shake the dust of it off your feet.
Jesus's advice to the disciples
Gospel of St Matthew

I found my mind wandering at games; loved boxing and was good at it; and in summer, having chosen rowing instead of cricket, lay peacefully by the Stour, well upstream of the rhythmic creaking and the exhortation, reading *Lily Christine* and Gibbon and gossiping with kindred lotus-eaters under the willow branches.
Patrick Leigh Fermor

We are now threatened with the prospect of our being only consumers, able to consume anything from any point in the world and from any culture, but of losing all originality.
Claude Lévi-Strauss

It doesn't matter if I'm only to be gone four days, as in this case; I take six months' supply of reading material everywhere. Anyone who needs further explication of this eccentricity can find it usefully set out in the first pages of Somerset Maugham's story 'The Book-Bag'.
Robin McKinley

Only by going alone in silence, without baggage, can one truly get into the heart of the wilderness. All other travel is mere dust and hotels and baggage and chatter.
John Muir

If you are a fast reader, you will probably run out of books, however many you take. In far-off places they can be more precious than gold and it is a good idea to be alert for swopping opportunities from the moment you have finished your first book. Be careful not to be the loser in the swopping deals; I always start the journey with an impeccable selection of books, but usually end up with *The Macrobiotic Way to Health*, *Das Kapital* and *Dramidion: a story of love on the planet Mars*.

John Hatt

Hotels? – they reek of the nastiest sort of affluence.
Dervla Murphy

I'd pay £10,000 not to set foot on a cruise ship. Really. It would be my worst nightmare.
Dervla Murphy

He that is a traveller must have the back of an ass to bear all, a tongue like the tail of a dog to flatter all, the mouth of a hog to eat what is set before him, the ear of a merchant to hear all and say nothing.
Thomas Nashe

'God has given us the Papacy,' the thirty-seven-year-old pope [Leo X] is said to have written to his brother Giuliano soon after his accession. 'Now let us enjoy it.'
John Julius Norwich

If you wish to travel far and fast, travel light. Take off all your envies, jealousies, unforgiveness, selfishness and fears.
Cesare Pavese

My father always taught me to buy the first round of drinks at a bar. Partly out of good manners, but partly because it leaves you with the freedom to leave.

Barnaby Rogerson

The lust of avarice has so totally seized upon mankind that their wealth seems rather to possess them than they possess their wealth.
Pliny

They never taste who always drink:
they always talk, who never think.
Matthew Prior

A traveller without observation is a bird without wings.
Saadi

There is only one happiness in this life, to love and be loved.
George Sand

> Only when the last tree has died and the last river
> has been poisoned and the last fish has been caught
> will we realise that we cannot eat money.
> *Chief Seattle*

Never so happy as in old clothes and with no watch
but his belly.
Frank Tatchell

> Gin is better in the tropics than whisky
> and rum is the wholesomest drink at sea.
> *Frank Tatchell*

Luxury is the enemy of observation, a costly indulgence
that induces such a good feeling that you notice nothing.
Paul Theroux

> 'Why are you packing all that?
> We're only going for two or three months.'
> *Wilfred Thesiger, seeing his travelling companion*
> *packing a spare shirt and a toothbrush.*

What a strange illusion it is to suppose that beauty is goodness.
Leo Tolstoy

> Life is short. Break the rules. Forgive quickly.
> Kiss slowly. Love truly. Laugh uncontrollably and
> never regret anything that makes you smile.
> *Mark Twain*

If your group are becoming bored of travelling, or of each other, organise a picnic lunch. Send one or two out with the local guide to forage for the freshest and ripest tomatoes, melons, cucumbers, cheese, fruit, sweetmeats, and bread hot from the oven. At the last minute, stop at a kebab shop for some köfte straight from the grill.

Antony Wynn

In character, in manner, in style, in all things,
the supreme excellence is simplicity.
Henry Wadsworth Longfellow

FOUR

Encounters with the Unknown

To move, to breath, to fly, to float. To gain all while you give.
To roam the roads of lands remote. To travel is to live.
Hans Christian Andersen

> One doesn't discover new lands without consenting
> to lose sight of the shore for a very long time.
> *André Gide*

I don't believe in magic, the young boy said.
The old man smiled, you will, when you see her.
Atticus

> 'I have never planned anything illegal in my life,'
> Aunt Augusta said. 'How could I plan anything of the
> kind when I have never read any of the laws
> and have no idea what they are?'
> *Aunt Augusta, from Graham Greene's* Travels with My Aunt

I have felt the wind on the wings of madness.
Charles Baudelaire

> Every hundred feet the world changes.
> *Roberto Bolaño*

Half the fun of travel is the aesthetic of lostness.
Ray Bradbury

**Travelling outgrows its motives. It soon proves
sufficient in itself. You think you are making a trip,
but soon it is making you… or unmaking you.**
Nicolas Bouvier

When we die, the wind blows away our footprints.
Bushmen from the Kalahari

I depart,
Whither I know not; but the hour's gone by,
When Albion's lessening shores could grieve or glad mine eye.
Lord Byron

The only way of catching a train I ever discovered is to miss
the train before.
G K Chesterton

I am prepared for the worst but hope for the best.
Benjamin Disraeli

Prepare well and keep an open mind.
Georgia de Chamberet

**Like all great travellers, I have seen more
than I can remember, and remember more
than I have seen.**
Benjamin Disraeli

The sun made me an Arab but never warped me to orientalism.
Charles Doughty

Do not follow where the path may lead.
Go instead where there is no path and leave a trail.
Ralph Waldo Emerson

You never know what to expect on encountering royalty. I've
seen 'em stark naked except for wings of peacock feathers
(Empress of China), giggling drunk in the embrace of a
wrestler (Maharani of the Punjab), voluptuously wrapped
in wet silk (Queen of Madagascar), wafting to and fro on a
swing (Rani of Jhansi), and tramping along looking like an
out-of-work charwoman (our own gracious monarch).
Flashman (George Macdonald Fraser)

I was alive to the possibility of disaster;
but was betting on complete fiasco.
Peter Fleming

Adventures do occur, but not punctually.
E M Forster

The madman is a dreamer awake.
Sigmund Freud

In three words I can sum up everything I've learned about life: it goes on.
Robert Frost

A journey is a gesture inscribed in space, it vanishes even as it's made. You go from one place to another place, and on to somewhere else again, and already behind you there is no trace that you were ever there.
Damon Galgut

Happiness always looks small while you hold it in your hands, but let it go and you learn at once how big and precious it is.
Maxim Gorky

I now know, by an almost fatalistic conformity with the facts, that my destiny is to travel.
Ernesto 'Che' Guevara

There's always something suspect about an intellectual on the winning side.
Václav Havel

Nothing endures but change.
Heraclitus

Any moment might be our last. Everything is more
beautiful because we're doomed. You will never be lovelier
than you are now. We will never be here again.
Homer

For I know well in my gut and in my heart,
A day will come when Sacred Troy will perish,
And Priam of the good lance, and all his people will be slain.
Hector in The Illiad, *quoted by Scipio after he had sacked
Carthage. Polybius, who overheard him, knew he was
imagining the fall of Rome.*

They don't travel because they could get sick,
they don't go out because they could be robbed,
they don't live because they could die.
Rudyard Kipling

Either I can be like some traveller of the olden days, who was faced with a stupendous spectacle, all, almost all of which eluded him, or filled him with scorn and disgust; or I can be a modern traveller, chasing after the vestiges of a vanished reality... A few hundred years hence, in this same place another traveller, as despairing as myself, will mourn the disappearance of what I might have seen, but failed to.
Claude Lévi-Strauss

I know there is no straight road,
No straight road on this world,
Only a giant labyrinth
Of intersecting crossroads.
Federico García Lorca

You do not travel if you are afraid of the unknown, you travel for the unknown, that reveals you with yourself.
Ella Maillart

Never hesitate to go far away, beyond all seas,
all frontiers, all countries, all beliefs.
Amin Maalouf

The more I travelled the more I realized that fear makes strangers of people who should be friends.
Shirley MacLaine

Disregard all advice against going on a long and potentially dangerous journey by camel. The naysayers can stay at their desks writing emails to each other. You are embarking on a life-changing, life-enhancing expedition. They are not.
Justin Marozzi

But at my back I always hear
Time's wingèd chariot hurrying near;
And yonder all before us lie
Deserts of vast eternity.
Andrew Marvell

Trust in God but tie your camel first.
The Prophet Muhammad

He who fears he shall suffer, already suffers what he fears.
Montaigne

My ideal unplanned existence – travelling, reading and writing, not knowing what was going to happen next year or next month or even next week.
Dervla Murphy

Choose your country, identify the areas most frequented by tourists – and then go in the opposite direction.
Dervla Murphy

You can handle just about anything that comes at you out on the road with a believable grin, common sense and whiskey.
Bill Murray

Let others praise ancient times:
I am glad I was born in these.
Ovid

The secret to happiness is freedom.
And the secret to freedom is courage.
Pericles

Grief has limits, whereas apprehension has none.
For we grieve only for what we know has happened,
but we fear all that possibly may happen.
Pliny

In these matters the only certainty is that nothing is certain.
Pliny

Be free, and scorn to have our free-born toe
Dragooned into a wooden shoe.
Matthew Prior

Always look into the eyes of those you are talking to. Never place your trust with anyone who talks to you whilst wearing dark glasses; you can lie with your face, but not with your eyes.

Barnaby Rogerson

You don't choose the day you enter the world and you don't chose the day you leave. It's what you do in between that makes all the difference.
Anita Septimus

You'll get mixed up, of course, as you already know.
You'll get mixed up with many strange birds as you go.
So be sure when you step,
Step with care and great tact, and remember that life's
A Great Balancing Act.
Dr Seuss

Hell is empty and all the devils are here.
William Shakespeare

**A ship in harbour is safe, but that is not what
ships are built for.**
John A Shedd

We English rely for success almost desperately on the breaking of rules, and it will be a poor day when we forget to do so.
Freya Stark

Without a local guide, it can only ever be all about you.
Matthew Teller

A journey is like marriage.
The certain way to be wrong
is to think you control it.
People don't take trips …
trips take people.
John Steinbeck

We travel together, passengers on a little spaceship, dependent on its vulnerable reserves of air and soil, all committed, for our safety, to its security and peace. Preserved from annihilation only by the care, the work and the love we give our fragile craft.
Adlai Stevenson

Every exit is an entry to somewhere else.
Tom Stoppard

Life is short and the world is wide.
Frank Tatchell

Take a Petzl head torch. At the bottom of the pack. For that moment when you get lost at the end of a day's trekking.
Hugh Thomson

> Don't be paranoid – much better to be open and full
> of trust with people. And the ones who are paranoid
> always get mugged anyway.
>
> *Hugh Thomson*

Most travel, and certainly the rewarding kind, involves depending
on the kindness of strangers, putting yourself into the hands of
people you don't know and trusting them with your life.
Paul Theroux

> Tourists don't know where they've been,
> travellers don't know where they're going.
> *Paul Theroux*

I went to the woods because I wished to live deliberately,
to front only the essential facts of life, and see if I could
not learn what it had to teach, and not, when I came to die,
discover that I had not lived.
Henry David Thoreau

> A journey is not a cure. It brings an illusion, only,
> of change, and becomes at best a spartan comfort.
> *Colin Thubron*

> A smile helps.
>
> *Sara Wheeler*

**Do the thing you fear most
and the death of fear is certain.**
Mark Twain

Climate is what we expect, weather is what we get.
Mark Twain

A good traveller has no fixed
plans and is not intent on
arriving.
Lao Tzu

Not I, not anyone else, can travel that road for you,
You must travel it for yourself.
Walt Whitman

All women become like their mothers. That is their tragedy.
No man does. That's his.
Oscar Wilde

Tips have their value, but there is nothing as gratifying
and edifying as making all the mistakes yourself and
surviving.

Isambard Wilkinson

FIVE

Humility and Tolerance

**I despise no-one, she said, no-one. Regret your own
actions, if you like that kind of wallowing in self-pity,
but never, never despise. Never presume yours
is the better morality.**
Aunt Augusta, from Graham Greene's Travels with My Aunt

You aspire to great things? Begin with little ones.
St Augustine

It was pride that turned angels into devils, it is humility that
makes men as angels.
St Augustine

Forgive many things in others, nothing in yourself.
Ausonius

There is a pleasure in the pathless woods,
There is a rapture on the lonely shore,
There is society, where none intrudes,
By the deep Sea, and music in its roar:
I love not Man the less, but Nature more.
Lord Byron

When I went South I never meant to write a book: I rather despised those who did so as being of an inferior breed to those who did things and said nothing about them.
Apsley Cherry-Garrard

If you drink the water of another country,
obey another country's laws.
Traditional Chinese saying

Strength is just an accident arising from the
weakness of others.
Joseph Conrad

My body has certainly wandered a good deal, but I have an
uneasy suspicion that my mind hasn't wondered enough.
Noel Coward

Patriotism is a kind of religion;
it is the egg from which wars
are hatched.
Guy de Maupassant

Two things are infinite: the universe and human stupidity;
and I'm not sure about the universe.
Albert Einstein

The world is good enough for me,
if only I can be good enough for it.
William Empson

Experience, travel – these are as education in themselves.
Euripides

We are as liable to be corrupted by
books as we are by companions.
Henry Fielding

Travel makes one modest. You see what
a tiny place you occupy in the world.
Gustave Flaubert

I didn't write. I just wandered about.
Martha Gellhorn

**Any fool can make something complicated.
It takes a genius to make it simple.**
Woody Guthrie

Anyone who takes himself too seriously always runs the risk of looking ridiculous; anyone who can consistently laugh at himself does not.
Václav Havel

There is nothing more admirable than when two people who see eye to eye keep house as man and wife, confounding their enemies and delighting their friends.
Homer

You cannot fly like an eagle with the wings of a wren.
W H Hudson

There is only one corner of the world you can be certain of improving, and that's yourself.
Aldous Huxley

The actions of men are the best interpreters of their thoughts.
James Joyce

The first thing we see as we travel round the world is our own filth, thrown into the face of mankind.
Claude Lévi-Strauss

> Never turn your nose up at the local food, no matter how much you like fish and chips.
>
> *Dmetri Kakmi*

The world began without man and it will complete itself without him.
Claude Lévi-Strauss

If you reject the food, ignore the customs, fear the religion and avoid the people, you might better stay home.
James Michener

To succeed in this world one should seem a fool, but be wise.
Montesquieu

Strong bonds are forged in high emotional temperatures.
Dervla Murphy

Man is neither an angel nor a brute, but the unfortunate twist to the matter is that the cause of the angels is only ever applied with brute force.
Pascal

No one should be ashamed to admit they are wrong, which is but saying, in other words, that they are wiser today than they were yesterday.
Alexander Pope

Praise undeserved, is satire in disguise.
Alexander Pope

'Tis remarkable that they talk most who have the least to say.
Matthew Prior

The mark of the immature man is that he wants to die nobly
for a cause, while the mark of the mature man is that he
wants to live humbly for one.
J D Salinger

I'm sick of not having the courage to be an absolute nobody.
J D Salinger

Take only memories, leave only footprints.
Chief Seattle

Aboard, aboard for shame
Give every man thy ear but few thy voice
Take each man's censure but reserve thy judgement..
Neither a lender nor a borrower be,
For loan oft loses both itself and friend...
This above all, to thine own self be true,
and it shall follow as the night the day,
thou cannot then be false to any man.
Polonius's advice to Laertes as he pushes him
aboard his boat in *Hamlet*
William Shakespeare

Nothing wilts faster than laurels that have been rested upon.
Percy Bysshe Shelley

A traveller respects the conventions of the people of the land, lives quietly as they do, speaks the language as well as they are able and sincerely admires their good qualities.
Frank Tatchell

The men simply did what [bush]men do without making anything of it, and didn't even think of themselves as brave.
Elizabeth Marshall Thomas

Men have become the tools of their tools.
Henry David Thoreau

Whenever you find yourself on the side of the majority, it is time to pause and reflect.
Mark Twain

If God had really intended men to fly,
he'd make it easier to get to the airport.
George Winters

Those who have much are often greedy.
Those who have little always share.
Oscar Wilde

SIX

Healing and Enlightenment

Adventure is worthwhile.
Aristotle

> *Solvitur ambulando* – It is solved by walking.
> *St Augustine*

'Are you really a Roman Catholic?' I asked my aunt with
interest. She replied promptly and seriously, 'Yes, my dear,
only I just don't believe in all the things they believe in.'
Aunt Augusta, from Graham Greene's Travels with My Aunt

Several years went by before I could relax in that living plexus
for which even now I have no name; but only when at last
relaxed could I see the possibilities of a life in which to be
deprived of Europe was not to be deprived of too much.
Cabeza de Vaca

> I have wandered all my life, and I have also travelled;
> the difference between the two being this, that we wander
> for distraction, but we travel for fulfilment.
> *Hilaire Belloc*

One of the gladdest moments of human life is the departure upon a distant journey into unknown lands. Shaking off with one mighty effort the fetters of habit, the leaden weight of routine, the cloak of many cares and the slavery of home, man feels once more happy.
Richard Burton

Walking is a virtue, tourism a deadly sin.
Bruce Chatwin

If you love your son, you must let him travel.
Traditional Chinese saying

When a man starts talking to you about progress, he wants to make you his slave.
Albert Cossery

Once a year, go somewhere you have never been before.
Dalai Lama

'There is no fire in hell,' he reported. 'Everyone who goes there brings their own fire, and their own pain, from this world.'
William Dalrymple

Don't get up early to avoid the crowds at big sites. Instead, get to the site an hour or two before it closes. You'll find relative solitude and the best of the light.

Rupert Smith

'Hope' is the thing with
             feathers
That perches in the soul,
And sings the tune without
             the words,
And never stops, at all
Emily Dickinson

In a rich man's house there is no place to spit but his face.
Diogenes

The cleverest of all is the man who calls himself a fool at least
once a month.
Fyodor Dostoyevsky

One father is more than a hundred schoolmasters.
George Herbert

Seize the day, and put the least possible trust in tomorrow.
Horace

One curiosity of being a foreigner everywhere is that one finds
oneself discerning Edens where the locals see only Purgatory.
Pico Iyer

Your time is limited, so don't waste it living someone else's life. Don't be trapped by dogma – which is living with the results of other people's thinking. Don't let the noise of other's opinions drown out your own inner voice. And most important, have the courage to follow your heart and intuition. They somehow already know what you truly want to become. Everything else is secondary.
Steve Jobs

> I never desire to converse with a man
> who has written more than he has read.
> *Samuel Johnson*

Until now I had clung to the comforting belief that human beings eventually come to terms with sorrow and pain. Now I understood I was wrong, and like Paul I suffered a conversion – but to pessimism. These little girls, any one of whom could be my daughter, came into the restaurant weeping, and they were weeping when they were led away. I knew that, condemned to ever-lasting darkness, hunger and loss, they would weep incessantly. They would never recover from their pain, and I would never recover from the memory of it.
Norman Lewis

> There are no foreign lands.
> It is the traveller only who is foreign.
> *Robert Louis Stevenson*

Boy, those French.
They have a different word for everything.
Steve Martin

Running water is sweet but standing pools stink; take away idleness, and the bait of all vice is taken away. Men were created to move, as birds to fly; what they learn by nature, that reason joined to nature teacheth us.
Fynes Moryson

Art does this because it stays with us as an intimation that Love has power and the world makes sense.
Iris Murdoch

Tell me who is travelled in history, what good poet is or ever was there, who hath not a little spice of wantonness in his days?
Thomas Nashe

Freedom is the sure possession of those alone who have the courage to defend it.
Pericles

All are but parts of one stupendous whole, whose body Nature is, and God the soul.
Alexander Pope

Keep a patch of sky above your life.
Marcel Proust

I believe that I am in Hell, therefore I am.
Arthur Rimbaud

We are our choices.
Jean-Paul Sartre

But, good gracious, you've got to educate him first. You can't expect a boy to be vicious until he's been to a good school.
Saki

Travel and change of place impart new vigour to the mind.
Seneca

All of us who are worth anything, spend our manhood in unlearning the follies, or expiating the mistakes, of our youth.
Percy Bysshe Shelley

If you want the present to be different from the past, study the past.
Spinoza

Do not overdo the walking, let fifteen miles a day be your maximum.
Frank Tatchell

You think of travellers as bold, but our guilty secret is that travel is one of the laziest ways on earth of passing the time.
Paul Theroux

An early-morning walk is a blessing for the whole day.
Henry David Thoreau

A nation is bound not only by the real past, but the stories it tells itself: by what it remembers and what it forgets.
Colin Thubron

I have two doctors, my left leg and my right.
George Trevelyan

Kindness is the language which the deaf can hear and the blind can see.
Mark Twain

Golf is a grand walk spoiled.
Mark Twain

I read; I travel; I become.
Derek Walcott

Religion is like a blind man looking in a black room
for a black cat that isn't there, and finding it.
Oscar Wilde

SEVEN

Monotony and Excitement

Now and then it is good
to pause in our pursuit of
happiness and just be happy.
Apollinaire

Sometimes I have an awful feeling that I am the only one left
anywhere who finds any fun in life.
Aunt Augusta, from *Graham Greene's* Travels with My Aunt

A day trip is always too long and too short.
Sybille Bedford

There are probably few accessible places on the face of the
globe where one can get less comfort for one's money than
the Sahara.
Paul Bowles

I am awfully greedy; I want everything from life. I want to be a woman and to be a man, to have many friends and to have loneliness, to work much and write good books, to travel and enjoy myself, to be selfish and to be unselfish… You see, it is difficult to get all that I want. And then when I do not succeed I get mad with anger.
Simone de Beauvoir

All the earth is scarred with roads, and all the sea furrowed with the tracks of ships, and over all the roads and all the waters a continuous stream of people passes up and down – travelling, as they say, for their pleasure. What is it, I wonder, that they go out to see?
Gertrude Bell

In the end, the bedrock of existence is not made up of the family, or work, or what others say or think of you, but of moments like this when you are exalted by a transcendent power that is more serene than love. Life dispenses them parsimoniously: our feeble hearts could not stand more.
Nicolas Bouvier

To my mind, the greatest reward and luxury of travel is to be able to experience everyday things as if for the first time, to be in a position in which almost nothing is so familiar it is taken for granted.
Bill Bryson

> And why not? The mind of man is capable of anything – because everything is in it, all the past as well as all the future.
> *Joseph Conrad*

So much beauty in the world, so few eyes that see it.
Albert Cossery

I think that travel comes from some deep urge to see the world, like the urge that brings up a worm in an Irish bog to see the moon when it is full.
Lord Dunsany

> Gradually the magic of the island [Corfu] settled over us as gently and clingingly as pollen.
> *Gerald Durrell*

Life is like riding a bicycle. To keep your balance, you must keep moving.
Albert Einstein

> Traveling tends to magnify all human emotions.
> *Peter Hoeg*

On Travel and the Journey Through Life

One is reminded, at a level deeper than all words,
how making a living and making a life sometimes
point in opposite directions.
Pico Iyer

You may live in a place for months, even years, and it does not
touch you, but a weekend or a night in another, and you feel
as if your whole being has been sprayed with an equivalent of
a cosmic wind.
Doris Lessing

'Is there anybody there?' said the Traveller,
knocking on the moonlit door.
Walter de la Mare

I suppose sooner or later in
the life of everyone comes a
moment of trial. We all of us
have our particular devil who
rides us and torments us, and
we must give battle in the end.
Daphne du Maurier

It is not down in any map; true places never are.
Herman Melville

Stop worrying about the potholes in the road
and celebrate the journey.
Fitzhugh Mullan

**People from a planet without flowers would think
we must be mad with joy the whole time
to have such things about us.**
Iris Murdoch

We live in a wonderful world that is full of beauty, charm
and adventure. There is no end to the adventures we can
have if only we seek them with our eyes open.
Jawaharal Nehru

The whole Earth is the Sepulchre of famous men; and their
story is not graven only on Stone over their native earth, but
lives on far away, without visible symbol, woven into the stuff
of other men's lives.
Pericles

**An object in possession seldom retains the same charm
that it had in pursuit.**
Pliny

Nature is what mortals call God.
Pliny

**I did not fully understand the dread term
'terminal illness' until I saw Heathrow for myself.**
Dennis Potter

On Travel and the Journey Through Life

We have so separated ourselves, person from person and group from group, in the city, that we have made hatred a dreadfully easy emotion. It comes to us as lightly and insidiously as the symptoms of an unconsciously harboured disease.
Jonathan Raban

Modern travelling is not travelling at all;
it is merely being sent to a place, and
very little different from becoming a parcel.
John Ruskin

I am climbing a difficult road, but the glory gives strength.
Sextus Propertius

Oh, the places you'll go! There is fun to be done!
Dr Seuss

Why, then, the world's
mine oyster,
Which I with sword will open.
William Shakespeare

Travelling is one of the saddest pleasures of life.
Madame de Stael

To awaken alone in a strange town is one of the pleasantest sensations in the world.
Freya Stark

I travel a lot; I hate having my life disrupted by routine.
Caskie Stinnett

Travel is the frivolous part of serious lives,
and the serious part of frivolous ones.
Sophie Swetchine

Travel is glamorous only in retrospect.
Paul Theroux

One of the worst aspects of travelling with wealthy people, apart from the fact that the rich never listen, is that they constantly grouse about the high cost of living.
Paul Theroux

Carry a harmonica. You need to be able to play of course, but the inevitable longeurs of journeying will provide the time and solitude needed to practice. You can get from tortured wailing to agreeably listenable remarkably fast.
Jasper Winn

The most hazardous part of our expedition to Africa
was crossing Piccadilly Circus.
Joseph Thomson

There is nothing that is
comparable to it, as satisfactory
or as thrilling, as gathering the
vegetables one has grown.
Alice B Toklas

Normality is a paved road: it's comfortable to walk but no
flowers grow.
Vincent Van Gogh

Every man can transform the world from one of monotony
and drabness to one of excitement and adventure.
Irving Wallace

There are only two emotions in a plane: boredom and terror.
Orson Welles

**We are all in the gutter
but some of us are looking at the stars.**
Oscar Wilde

EIGHT

Journeys Without End and Homecomings

One's destination is never a place but a new way
of seeing things.
St Augustine

Whereas the tourist generally hurries back home at the end
of a few weeks or months, the traveller belonging no more
to one place than to the next, moves slowly over periods of
years, from one part of the earth to another. Indeed, he would
have found it difficult to tell, among the many places he had
lived, precisely where it was he had felt most at home.
Paul Bowles

It is better to travel well than to arrive.
Buddha

England, the only country in which I do not feel at home.
Richard Burton

Man's real home is not a house but the Road and …
life itself is a journey to be walked on foot.
Bruce Chatwin

On Travel and the Journey Through Life

Hope your road is a long one.
May there be many summer mornings when,
with what pleasure, what joy,
you enter harbours you're seeing for the first time;
…
But don't hurry the journey at all.
Better if it lasts for years,
so you're old by the time you reach the island,
wealthy with all you've gained on the way...
Cavafy

The whole object of travel is not to set foot on foreign land;
it is at last to set foot on one's own country as a foreign land.
G K Chesterton

If you have a garden and a library, you have everything you need.
Cicero

Every traveller has a home of his own, and he learns to
appreciate it the more from his wandering.
Charles Dickens

We shall not cease from exploration
And the end of all our exploring
Will be to arrive where we started
And know the place for the first time.
T S Eliot

Home is the place where, when you have to go there,
they have to take you in.
Robert Frost

A wise traveller never despises his own country.
Carlo Goldoni

The journey is the thing.
Homer

And if travel is like love, it is, in the end, mostly because it's a heightened state of awareness, in which we are mindful, receptive, undimmed by familiarity and ready to be transformed. That is why the best trips, like the best love affairs, never really end.
Pico Iyer

He made some reputation by travelling abroad but lost it all by travelling at home.
Samuel Johnson of 'Persian' Hanway

… crossing and recrossing the country every year, south in the winter and north in the summer and only because he has no place he can stay in without getting tired of it and because there's nowhere to go but everywhere, and keep rolling under the stars.
Jack Kerouac

It is good to have an end to journey toward, but it is the journey that matters in the end.
Ursula K Le Guin

All this, and discontent too! Otherwise, why am I sitting here dreaming of England? Why am I gazing at this campfire like a lost soul seeking a hope when all that I love is at my wingtips? Because I am curious. Because I am incorrigibly, now, a wanderer.
Beryl Markham

One's destination is never a place,
but a new way of seeing things.
Henry Miller

A man travels the world over in search of what he needs and returns home to find it.
George Moore

From the end spring new beginnings.
Pliny

Home is where the heart is.
Pliny

Who walks the fastest, but walks astray,
is only furthest from his way.
Matthew Prior

We do not receive wisdom, we must discover it for ourselves
after a journey that no one can take for us or spare us.
Marcel Proust

People who live on continents get into the habit of regarding
the ocean as journey's end, the full stop at the end of the
trek. For people who live on islands, the sea is always the
beginning. It's the ferry to the mainland, the escape route
from the boredom and narrowness of home.
Jonathan Raban

A great way to learn about your country is to leave it.
Henry Rollins

I dislike feeling at home when I am abroad.
George Bernard Shaw

I travel not to go anywhere, but
to go. I travel for travel's sake.
The great affair is to move.
Robert Louis Stevenson

On Travel and the Journey Through Life

If you are ready to leave father and mother, brother and sister, and wife and child and friends, and never see them again: if you have paid your debts, and made your will, and settled all your affairs, and are a free man: then you are ready for a walk.
Henry David Thoreau

Journeys begin long before their first step is taken…
Colin Thubron

It is easy to go down to Hell: night and day, the dark gates of death stand wide open: but to climb back again, to retrace your steps and return to the clear air and light, there's the task.
Virgil

With languages, you are at home anywhere.
Edmund De Waal

There is one voyage, the first, the last, the only one.
Thomas Wolfe

As a woman I have no country.
As a woman I want no country.
As a woman, my country is the whole world.
Virginia Woolf

Don't bore people when you return.

Isambard Wilkinson

I travelled among unknown men,
In lands beyond the sea;
Nor, England! Did I know till then
What love I bore to thee.
William Wordsworth

No one realises how beautiful it is to travel until he comes
home and rests his head on his old, familiar pillow.
Lin Yutang

NINE

Writing and Travel

Of all possible subjects, travel is the most difficult for an artist, as it is the easiest for a journalist.
W H Auden

> I write because I am a writer. It is rather like cooking, to make something out of raw materials with your hands.
> *Sybille Bedford*

I wish I had written more books and spent less time being in love. It is very difficult doing both at the same time...
so much siesta and dining out and never any work.
Sybille Bedford

> Novels among other things are galleries of mirrors.
> *Sybille Bedford*

What is a travel book? For me it is the story of what happened to one particular person in a particular place, and nothing more than that.
Paul Bowles

No, no! The adventures first,
explanations take such a dreadful time.
Lewis Carroll

As a journalist use your feet. Never compose a story from telephone, text or telegram. Talk to everyone, face to face. Take nothing from PR people aside from a drink. Be irreverent to the powerful, most especially prime ministers and presidents.
Barbara Cartland

Better to write for yourself and have no public,
than to write for the public and have no self.
Cyril Connolly

If I couldn't walk fast and far, I should just explode.
Charles Dickens

You are never lonely with a book.
Marlene Dietrich

Never complain, never explain.
Benjamin Disraeli

If you can't explain it to a six year old,
you don't understand it yourself.
Albert Einstein

The machinations of ambiguity are among the very roots of poetry.
William Empson

83

> Writing is, in the end, that oddest of anomalies:
> an intimate letter to a stranger.
> *Pico Iyer*

He that would travel for the entertainment of others, should remember that the great object of remark is human life. Every nation has something peculiar in its manufactures, its works of genius, its medicines, its agriculture, its customs, and its policy. He only is a useful traveller, who brings home something by which his country might be benefited, who procures some supply of want, or some mitigation of evil, which may enable his readers to compare their condition with that of others, to improve it whenever it is worse, and whenever it is better to enjoy it.
Samuel Johnson

A writer just starts a book – a reader finishes it.
Samuel Johnson

Misery, anger, indignation, discomfort – these conditions produce literature. Contentment never. So there you are.
T E Lawrence

> I can understand the mad passion for travel books
> and their deceptiveness. They create the illusion of
> something which no longer exists but still should exist.
> *Claude Lévi-Strauss*

I would rather cross the African continent again than write another book. It is far easier to travel than to write about it.
David Livingstone

It has all the normal stigmata of the travel book, the fake intensities, the tendency to discover the soul of a town after spending two hours in it, the boring descriptions of conversations with taxi drivers.
George Orwell
reviewing Henry Miller's *The Colossus of Maroussi*

> The fortunate man is he to whom the gods have
> granted the power to write what is worth recording,
> or to write what is worth reading, and most
> fortunate of all is the man who can do both.
> *Pliny*

Pensive poets painful vigils keep
Sleepless themselves to give their readers sleep
Alexander Pope

> Literature is made out of the misfortune of others.
> A large number of travel books fail simply because
> of the monotonous good luck of their authors.
> *V S Pritchett*

If we live inside a bad joke, it is up to us to learn,
at best and worst, to tell it well.
Jonathan Raban

When travelling, I usually keep a notebook: when home at my desk, the notebook serves mainly to remind me how little I saw at the time, or rather how I was noticing the wrong things. But the notes do spur memories, and it's the memories that I trust. The wine stain on the page may tell me more than the words there, which usually strike me as hopelessly inadequate.
Jonathan Raban

Life, as the most ancient of all metaphors insists, is a journey: and the travel book, in its deceptive simulation of the journey's fits and starts, rehearses life's own fragmentation. More even than the novel, it embraces the contingency of things.
Jonathan Raban

> An artist's only concern is to shoot for some kind of perfection, and on his own terms, not anyone else's.
> *J D Salinger*

I think what stands for travel writing stands for all sorts of writing – and that is, it's not just about describing where you are, it's about understanding it and your relation to it.
Antony Sattin

> My father used to say that stories are part of the most precious heritage of mankind.
> *Tahir Shah*

Heading south in my usual travelling mood – hoping for the picturesque, expecting misery, braced for the appalling.
Paul Theroux

The worst trips make the best reading.
Paul Theroux

A person who won't read has no
advantage over one who can't.
Mark Twain

Why did I write? Because I found life unsatisfactory.
Tennesse Williams

Escape, surprise, discovery and transformation
is the great strength of travel writing.
James Whitfield

Travel writing is the ideal vehicle for the humanist, the
eccentric, the loner or the crackpot, who fitted into no easy
political or intellectual scheme.
James Whitfield

I never travel without my diary. One should always have
something sensational to read in the train.
Oscar Wilde

TEN

Wise Tweets for a Postcard Home

There is no saint without a past,
no sinner without a future.
St Augustine

Always laugh when you can, it is cheap medicine.
Lord Byron

The traveller sees what he sees, the tourist sees what he has
come to see.
G K Chesterton

Outside of the bedroom, a husband and wife
should treat each other like guests.
Traditional Chinese saying

Tolerant men are never stupid,
and stupid men are never tolerant.
Traditional Chinese saying

Television is for appearing on, not for looking at.
Noel Coward

The belief in a supernatural source of evil is not necessary; men alone are quite capable of every wickedness.
Joseph Conrad

Oh, don't let's wish for the moon. We've already got the stars.
Bette Davis

It is the friends you can call up at four in the morning that matter.
Marlene Dietrich

I do not know whether there are gods, but there ought to be.
Diogenes

Youth is blunder, manhood a struggle, old age a regret.
Benjamin Disraeli

Science without religion is lame, religion without science is blind.
Albert Einstein

The heart of standing is that you cannot fly.
William Empson

'Twixt devil and deep sea, man hacks his cave.
William Empson

Everywhere I go, I find a poet has been there before me.
Sigmund Freud

The weak can never forgive.
Forgiveness is the attribute of the strong.
Mahatma Gandhi

The country is calm. Calm as a morgue or a grave.
Václav Havel

Paris is always a good idea.
Audrey Hepburn

**Is he not sacred, even to the gods,
the wandering man who comes in weariness?**
Homer

Liberties are not given, they are taken.
Aldous Huxley

Fire on the mountain: the image of the wanderer.
I Ching

Serendipity was my tour guide, assisted by caprice.
Pico Iyer

If life is a journey then let my soul travel and share your pain.
Santosh Kalwar

I feel about airplanes the way I feel about diets. It seems to
me that they are wonderful things for other people to go on.
Jean Kerr

Trivial things light fuses in the memory.
Paddy Leigh Fermor

I wish I was a woman of about thirty-six,
dressed in black satin with a string of pearls.
Daphne du Maurier

Perhaps when distant people on other planets pick up some
wavelength of ours all they hear is a continuous scream.
Iris Murdoch

Poverty denotes a lack of necessities,
simplicity a lack of needs.
Dervla Murphy

Free speech is my right to say what you don't want to hear.
George Orwell

Too fucking busy and vice versa.
Dorothy Parker

There is always something new out of Africa.
Pliny

In an underdeveloped country don't drink the water. In a developed country don't breathe the air.
Jonathan Raban

Genius is the recovery of childhood at will.
Arthur Rimbaud

Vanity is the quicksand of reason.
George Sand

Fear not for the future, weep not for the past.
Percy Bysshe Shelley

What Paul says about Peter tells us more about Paul than about Peter.
Spinoza

A lie can travel halfway around the world while the truth is putting on its shoes.
Charles Spurgeon

True fun in life consists in doing things –
not in having them.
Frank Tatchell

Everyone thinks of changing the world,
but no one thinks of changing himself.
Leo Tolstoy

If you don't read the newspaper you are uninformed;
if you do read the newspaper you are misinformed.
Mark Twain

Against the assault of laughter, nothing can stand.
Mark Twain

While armchair travellers dream of going places, traveling armchairs dream of staying put.
Anne Tyler

You only live once, but if you do it right, once is enough.
Mae West

Sex is emotion in motion.
Mae West

I am as bad as the worst, but thank God, as good as the best.
Walt Whitman

> The best revenge is to live well.
> *Oscar Wilde*

The violets in the mountains have broken the rocks.
Tennessee Williams

Biographical Sketches

Hans Christian Andersen (1805–75)
Danish author famed for his literary fairy tales, which have become embedded in the West's collective consciousness and have inspired ballets, plays and films.

Maya Angelou (1928–2014)
American poet, memoirist and civil rights activist, best known for her series of autobiographies which focus on her childhood and early adult experiences. She worked with Martin Luther King Jr. and Malcolm X on the civil rights movement and lectured around the country. She recited her poem 'On the Pulse of the Morning' at the first inauguration of Bill Clinton.

Guillaume Apollinaire (1880–1918)
French poet, playwright, art critic and novelist, admired from an early age for the originality of his poetry. He is credited with coining the term 'cubism' to describe the emerging art form in 1911. Wounded in World War I, he died two years later of Spanish flu.

Aristotle (384–322 BCE)
Greek philosopher and polymath who was taught by Plato and founded The Lyceum, where a Peripatetic school of philosophy flourished. His philosophy exerts an influence on every form of knowledge in the West. Little is known about his life but he left Athens to tutor Alexander the Great in 343 BCE. Some of his zoological observations, such as the reproductive arm of the octopus, were disbelieved until the 19th century.

Atticus

Atticus is an anonymous Canadian who started posting poetry online in 2013 and went on to have two bestselling collections of poetry. When he reads or signs books, he wears a mask. Proceeds benefit mental health awareness charities.

W H Auden (1907–73)

British-American poet noted for his stylistic and technical achievement, engaging with politics, morals, love and religion. His first book, *Poems*, brought him wide public attention at the age of twenty-three. Auden was a prolific writer of prose essays and reviews, regarded by some as a lesser Yeats and Eliot, by others as the greatest mind of the 20th century.

Aunt Augusta

The fictional, eccentric aunt and travelling companion of Henry Pulling, a retired bank manager in Graham Greene's novel *Travels with My Aunt* (1969). Aunt Augusta pulls Henry away from his quiet suburban existence into a world of adventure and crime.

Decius Magnus Ausonius (309–392 CE)

Ausonius's fame as a teacher of rhetoric led the Roman Emperor Valentinian to appoint him tutor to his son Gratian, who later made him consul. The death of his patrons, and the rise to power of the Christian Emperor Theodosius, encouraged Ausonius to return home to France to write.

Francis Bacon (1561–1626)

Francis Bacon was an important Elizabethan statesman, a scientist, philosopher and a brilliant essayist like his contemporary Montaigne.

James Baldwin (1924–87)

American writer and activist whose work dealt with fundamental personal and societal questions around masculinity, sexuality, race and class. His characters were often African-American and gay, facing internal and external obstacles in their search for social and self-acceptance. He continually fought for the civil rights of black people.

Buckaroo Banzai

The protagonist and eponymous scientist from the film *The Adventures of Buckaroo Banzai Across the 8th Dimension* (1984), who is tasked with saving the world. Despite doing poorly at the box office, the film has attracted a cult following once adapted for comics and games.

Rose Baring (b. 1961)

Rose learned Russian at school and later wrote the Cadogan Guide to Moscow and St Petersburg. She is the editor at Eland Publishing and has also trained as a psychoanalytic psychotherapist.

Amelia E Barr (1831–1919)

British novelist and teacher whose stories are set in Scotland and England, recalling memories from her childhood. In 1850 she moved to Illinois with her husband and set up a tutoring home for girls. After an accident which confined her to a chair, she started writing novels and stories.

Charles Baudelaire (1821–67)

French poet, essayist and art critic, Baudelaire was a master of rhyme and rhythm. He coined the term 'modernity', which later became synonymous with life in urban, industrial places. He was described as a dandy and a free spender, leading a hedonistic lifestyle.

Mary Ritter Beard (1876-1958)

An American historian, author and suffrage activist who was a lifelong advocate of social justice. She wrote *On Understanding Women* (1931), *America Through Women's Eyes* (Ed. 1933), and *Woman as Force in History: A Study in Traditions and Realities* (1946). Beard's interest in women's history led to her establishing the World Centre for Women's Archives in 1935.

Simone de Beauvoir (1908–86)
Leading radical figure of the French left – a philosopher, teacher, feminist historian, activist and writer. Her ground-breaking history of the oppression of women, *The Second Sex*, was first published in 1949.

Sybille Bedford (1911–2006)
German-born English writer of non-fiction and semi-autobiographical fiction much admired for her style. She mined her own life in her fiction, but also wrote a travel book about Mexico and was fascinated by the legal process and trials. She loved good food and wine.

Gertrude Bell (1868–1926)
English writer, traveller, archaeologist, Arabist and explorer who advised on Britain's imperial policy due to her knowledge of Syria, Palestine, Mesopotamia, Asia Minor and central Arabia. She played a major role in helping to administer the modern state of Iraq through her relations with tribal leaders.

Hilaire Belloc (1870–1953)
Franco-English writer and historian whose Catholic faith made its way into his poetry, satire and political activism. As a young man, he walked across the American Midwest, reciting poetry to ranch-owners in exchange for a bed. He ended his journey at his partner's home in California. Elodie Hogan became his wife and mother of their five children.

Wendell Berry (b. 1934)
American novelist, essayist, environmental activist and farmer. As an activist Berry has appeared at major conferences and written influential articles for the *New York Times* on preserving America's landscape and its political character. His nonfiction celebrates sustainable agriculture, healthy communities and frugality.

William Blake (1757–1827)
English poet, painter and printmaker who was largely

unrecognised during his life, but is now considered a seminal figure, best known for his prophetic works written in his idiosyncratic, distinctive style. He was a strong believer in spiritual freedom.

Roberto Bolaño (1953–2003)

Chilean writer, 'the most significant Latin American literary voice of his generation' (NYT), most famous for his posthumous novel *2666*. The son of a truck driver, he was brought up in Mexico but returned to Chile to aid the Allende revolution in 1973, was captured and held in custody. He lived in Spain in his later years.

Nicolas Bouvier (1929–98)

Swiss traveller, writer and photographer whose most famous works are *L'Usage du monde* (*The Way of the World*) and *Le Poisson-scorpion* (*The Scorpion-Fish*). His journey from Geneva to India was a major influence on the waves of travellers and hippies heading east in the 1960s and '70s.

Paul Bowles (1910–99)

American composer, author and translator who settled in Morocco for the best part of his life. He travelled the Sahara whilst working on his first novel, *The Sheltering Sky*, and used his subsequent fame to encourage Moroccan writers as well as transcribing and helping translate their stories.

Ray Bradbury (1920–2012)

American author and screenwriter famous for bringing fantasy into the literary mainstream. His story *The Homecoming* was picked from the slush-pile by Truman Capote, a young editorial assistant at the magazine *Mademoiselle* at the time, who liked his style.

Bill Bryson (b. 1951)

American-born British author of books on travel, the English language and science. He has been a resident of Britain for most of his life. He first came to fame in the UK with *Notes from a Small Island* (1995), which documented his travels around Britain. Born and raised in Iowa, he dropped out of university to backpack around Europe and met his wife whilst working in a psychiatric hospital in Surrey.

Buddha (c. 6th–4th centuries BCE)

An ascetic, religious leader and teacher who lived in India sometime between 6th–4th centuries BCE, he founded the world religion of Buddhism, pioneering meditative practices that combined sensual indulgence with strict asceticism.

Mikhail Bulgakov (1891–1940)

One of the great voices of Russian literature, whose most celebrated works include *The White Guard* and *The Master and Margarita*. Bulgakov was born in Kiev and trained to become a doctor but abandoned this profession in 1920 to better serve the Revolution as a journalist-writer.

Jackson Burnett

Jackson Burnett is the pen name of a writer and amateur fiddle player who lives in a Southwest American city where he practices law.

Richard Burton (1821–90)

British explorer, writer, scholar and soldier who reputedly spoke twenty-nine languages. He documented a journey he undertook to Mecca in disguise, at a time when Europeans were forbidden on pain of death. He translated *The Arabian Nights*, published the *Karma Sutra* in English and was the first European to visit the Great Lakes of Africa in search of the source of the Nile. He heavily criticised British imperialism in his writing.

George Gordon Byron (1788–1824)

One of the greatest English poets, Lord Byron was a leading figure in the Romantic movement. Among his most notable works is the long narrative poem *Don Juan*. He travelled extensively throughout Europe and died from fever whilst fighting with the Greeks against the Ottomans in the War of Independence.

Robert Byron (1905–41)

British travel writer, art critic and historian best known for his travelogue *The Road to Oxiana*. He found his subject in Persia and Afghanistan, where the architecture, landscape and culture inspired his very own form of travel narrative. He died in the Second World War, aged 35, going down in a ship bound for West Africa.

Álvar Núñez Cabeza de Vaca (c. 1488–c.1557)

Spanish explorer of the New World and one of the four survivors of the 1527 Narváez expedition. He was a trader and faith healer to North American tribes in what is now the US Southwest. After returning to Spain, he wrote an account of his journeys. He is considered a proto-anthropologist for his detailed accounts of the many tribes he encountered.

Tim Cahill (b. 1944)

American travel writer who, with professional long-distance driver Garry Sowerby, set a world record for speed driving the entire length of the American continent from Tierra del Fuego to Alaska, chronicled in his book *Road Fever*. Subsequent titles include *Pecked to Death by Ducks, Hold the Enlightenment* and *Jaguars Ripped my Flesh*.

Lewis Carroll (1832–98)

English author, poet and mathematician best known for *Alice's Adventures in Wonderland* (1865). He spent most of his life teaching at Christ Church, Oxford. The *Alice* of his great work was named after the daughter of the dean at Christ Church.

Barbara Cartland (1901–2000)

English writer best known for her prolific output of historical romance novels. Alongside Agatha Christie, she was one of the bestselling 20th-century authors worldwide. Often dressed in a pink chiffon gown, she was one of Britain's most popular media personalities.

C P Cavafy (1863–1933)

Greek poet, journalist and civil servant from Alexandria. His friend E M Forster introduced his work to the English-speaking world in 1923, describing him as 'a Greek gentleman in a straw hat, standing absolutely motionless at a slight angle to the universe'.

Georgia de Chamberet (b. 1964)

Born in Paris to an eccentric father and artistic mother, she worked as an editor at Quarto Books in the 1990s and went on to found the London-based literary agency BookBlast Ltd in 1997.

Bruce Chatwin (1940–89)

Chatwin's first job was at Sotheby's in London and he went on to write for the *Sunday Times Magazine*. In 1974 he went to Patagonia, partly in search of a real-life sloth, a piece of which he had found in his explorer-grandmother's house as a child. *In Patagonia* (1977) established Chatwin as a travel writer, but he considered himself a storyteller first, as evidenced by novels like *Utz* and *On the Black Hill*.

Apsley Cherry-Garrard (1886–1959)

English explorer of Antarctica and member of the Terra Nova expedition, which he documented in his book *The Worst Journey in the World* (1922). Impressed by his father's achievements in the British Army, Apsley felt he had to live up to them. He volunteered to join Scott's expedition and after being rejected twice, donated money and was taken on as an assistant zoologist. During an expedition to collect some Emperor Penguin's eggs, he and his companion experienced temperatures as low as -60.8°C and Apsley shattered his teeth from shuddering.

G K Chesterton (1874–1936)

English writer, philosopher and art critic whose fiction contained carefully concealed parables. A large man, he was known for his wit and his deliberate forgetfulness about where he was going.

Cicero (106–43BCE)

Roman statesman, lawyer, scholar and philosopher, who tried to uphold the principles of the Roman republic. He is one of Rome's greatest orators and prose stylists. After being proscribed an enemy of the state by Mark Antony, he was executed in 43 BC whilst trying to flee the Italian peninsula.

Charles Cooley (1864–1929)

American sociologist who came up with the concept of the 'looking-glass self', which asserted that a person's self grows out of society's influence.

Cyril Connolly (1903–74)

English literary critic and writer who edited the influential literary magazine *Horizon*. He wrote *Enemies of Promise*, a memoir which explored his failure as a writer whilst revealing some of his zest for life.

Joseph Conrad (1857–1924)

Polish-British writer regarded as one of the greatest novelists to write in the English language. He drew on his experiences of Poland and of his time serving in the French and British merchant navies to write about imperialism and colonialism. His novels often depict the trials of the human spirit in the face of an impassive universe.

Albert Cossery (1913–2008)

Egyptian-born writer who spent most of his life in Paris, although he set all of his books in Egypt or in an imaginary Middle Eastern country. His writings pay tribute to the misfits of his childhood in Cairo and praise a form of idleness unknown in our contemporary society. Born to a Greek Orthodox family of Syrian descent, in 60 years he only wrote eight novels (in French), in accordance with his philosophy that laziness is not a vice but a form of meditation.

Noel Coward (1899–1973)

English playwright, composer, director and actor known for his wit and flamboyance. He attended a dance academy as a child, making his stage début at the age of eleven. He wrote over 50 plays from his teens onwards. He did not publicly acknowledge his homosexuality, but his long-term partner, Graham Payne, published his diaries and letters posthumously.

Ralph Crawshaw (1921–2014)

Psychiatrist, author and activist who spent most of his life in Portland, Oregon. He set up numerous charities for medical research and was an environmental activist in his later years.

Dalai Lama (b. 1935)

The 14th and current Dalai Lama is Tenzin Gyatso, who lives as a refugee in India. The Dalai Lama is believed to be a reincarnation of the Bodhisattva of Compassion. He is a unifying symbol of the Tibetan state, working to overcome sectarianism in the exiled community. Tibet's self-declared independence from China was rejected in 1913 and still is today.

William Dalrymple (b. 1963)

Scottish-born historian who became a star travel writer straight out of university but subtly shifted his focus, after working as a journalist in Delhi, to become a narrative historian of India. He is also an art historian, photographer, a first-class raconteur and one of the co-founders of the Jaipur Festival. A selection of his recent books includes *Nine Lives: In Search of the Sacred in Modern India*, *Return of a King: The Battle for Afghanistan* 1839-42, while his most recent work is *Anarchy*, a history of the Indian subcontinent during the period 1739–1803.

Dante (1265–1321)

Dante Alighieri was an Italian poet, writer and philosopher. His *Divine Comedy* is one of the most important poems of the

Middle Ages. He established the use of vernacular in literature, until then only accessible to the most educated readers.

Bette Davis (1908–89)

American actress with a career spanning more than 50 years. She often played unsympathetic, sardonic characters and was known for her intense acting style and sometimes confrontational attitude on set, admitting herself that her acting success came at the expense of healthy personal relationships.

Walter de la Mare (1873–1956)

English poet, short story writer and novelist best remembered for his works for children, his poem 'The Listeners' and subtle psychological horror stories. He believed children were visionaries and saw his poetry coming from his childish self rather than his more mature, intellectual self.

Madame de Staël (1766–1817)

Anne Louise Germaine de Staël-Holstein was a French woman of letters and political theorist. She was the voice of moderation in the French Revolution and the Napoleonic era. As the first to notice Napoleon's tyrannical character, she was exiled and became the centre of the struggle against him.

Edmund De Waal (b. 1964)

Contemporary English artist, master potter and author, known for his large-scale installations of porcelain vessels. His novel, *The Hare with Amber Eyes*, told the story of his Jewish family and their collection of *netsuke*.

Charles Dickens (1812–70)

Great English Victorian novelist who created some of the world's best-known fictional characters. Like a character from one of his books, he left school at 12 to work in a boot-blacking factory after his father was incarcerated in a debtors' prison. He then worked as a journalist, wrote hundreds of short stories, fifteen novels and campaigned vigorously for children's rights and social reform.

Emily Dickinson (1830–86)

American poet whose vast and original body of work remained virtually unpublished in her lifetime, but was fortunately recognised by her sister. Emily had been well educated but lived all her life at a home dominated by her father, an autocratic New England lawyer-Congressman.

Marlene Dietrich (1901–92)

German-born American actress whose career began in 1920s Berlin, where she performed on stage and in silent films, rising to fame in *The Blue Angel* (1930). Her partnership with the director Von Sternberg over several films is hailed as one of the great collaborations in cinema history. She was known for her humanitarian efforts during World War II.

Diogenes (412–323 BCE)

A Greek philosopher who founded the philosophy of cynicism, Diogenes was a controversial figure who openly criticized the conventions of Athenian society. He led a deliberately simple life and described himself as cosmopolitan – a citizen of the world rather than of any one state. He made a virtue of poverty and notoriously sabotaged some of Plato's public lectures.

Benjamin Disraeli (1804–81)

British statesman and conservative politician who twice served as prime minister. Remembered for his influential voice on world affairs, Disraeli instigated a new era in Tory democracy and helped to expand the British Empire. Of Italian-Jewish origin, he also wrote novels.

Fyodor Dostoyevsky (1821–81)

One of the most influential figures of Russian literature, Dostoyevsky's early years were spent living in the grounds of a Moscow hospital where his father was a doctor. He was sentenced to death in 1849 for his radical socialism, though this was later commuted to exile in Siberia. His novels, including *The House of the Dead*, *Notes from Underground*, *Crime and Punishment* and *The Idiot*, are famous the world over.

Charles Doughty (1843–1926)

English poet, writer, explorer and traveller known for his two-volume book *Travels in Arabia Deserta* (1888) which, despite a cool reception, slowly became a touchstone of travel writing. It was rediscovered by T E Lawrence and republished in the 1920s.

Elizabeth Drew (b. 1935)

American political journalist and author who started out as Washington correspondent for *The Atlantic Monthly* and *The New Yorker* and became an important figure in American political reporting.

Daphne du Maurier (1907–89)

English novelist, biographer and playwright whose bestselling works were not at first taken seriously by critics, but have since earned a reputation for narrative craft. She spent much of her life in Cornwall, where most of her works are set. She was awarded Dame Commander of the British Empire in 1969, although she told no one about the honour, including her children.

Lord Dunsany (1878–1957)

Anglo-Irish writer and dramatist who lived in Ireland's longest inhabited home, Dunsany Castle near Tara, and worked with W B Yeats and Lady Gregory in supporting the Abbey Theatre. He was a chess and pistol champion, traveller and hunter.

Gerald Durrell (1925–95)

British naturalist, writer, zookeeper, conservationist and television presenter whose memoirs of his family's years living in Corfu have spawned two TV series. It was in Corfu that Durrell began collecting local fauna as pets. He worked in zoos in his 20s and eventually set up his own in Jersey, which acted as a reserve and regenerator for endangered species.

Albert Einstein (1879–1955)

German-Jewish theoretical physicist widely considered the most influential physicist of all time. He is best known for his theory of relativity and his contribution to quantum mechanics. He was awarded the Nobel Prize for physics in 1921. A US citizen by 1940, Einstein supported the allies against Nazi Germany during World War II.

T S Eliot (1888–1965)

Poet, publisher, playwright and literary critic, considered one of the 20th century's major poets and a central figure in Modernism. Born in St. Louis, Missouri, he moved to England in 1914 and renounced his US citizenship in 1927.

Ralph Waldo Emerson (1803–82)

American essayist, poet, lecturer, abolitionist and leader of the transcendentalist movement. He championed individualism and criticized the pressures of society, pursuing a life of teaching, lecturing and travelling. He was intent on the freeing of slaves from an early age.

William Empson (1906–84)

English literary critic and poet, widely influential for his practice of closely reading literary works. He is best known for his work *Seven Types of Ambiguity* (1930).

Euripides (480–406 BCE)

Tragedian of classical Athens who, along with Sophocles and Aeschylus, is one of three playwrights whose plays have survived in full. He innovated theatrical ideas by having mythical heroes portrayed as ordinary people in ordinary circumstances. He also became the most tragic of poets and a recluse, sleeping in a cave on Salamis, where a cult was established after his death.

Henry Fielding (1707–54)

An English novelist, satirist and dramatist. His most notable work is *Tom Jones*, a comic novel still widely appreciated today.

Fielding used his authority as a magistrate to establish London's first intermittently funded police force, the Bow Street Runners.

Flashman

Fictional cad created by George Macdonald Fraser in his series *The Flashman Papers*, first published in 1969. Harry Flashman is hurled into real historical events from 1839–94. Despite his cowardly nature, he finds himself in many dangerous situations and ends up influencing major turning points in history, meeting Wellington, Disraeli and Abraham Lincoln along the way.

Gustave Flaubert (1821–80)

French novelist known for his debut novel *Madame Bovary* (1857) and as mentor to the short-story writer Guy de Maupassant. He travelled to the Middle East in 1849, contracting syphilis in Beirut and other venereal diseases along the way. He was a pantheist and a flagrant supporter of any individual who protested against power and monopolies.

Peter Fleming (1907–71)

British adventurer, journalist, soldier and travel writer who was the elder brother of Ian, creator of James Bond. In 1932 Fleming joined an expedition to Brazil after answering an advertisement in the columns of *The Times*. He would later travel extensively through Asia, writing *One's Company* and *News from Tartary*.

E M Forster (1879–1970)

English novelist whose books examined class difference and hypocrisy and included *A Room with a View* (1908), *Howard's End* (1910) and *A Passage to India* (1924). He lived with his mother until the end of her life, and although never open about his homosexuality in death his ashes were mixed with those of one of his long-time lovers.

Anatole France (1844–1924)

Bestselling French writer who won the 1921 Nobel Prize in literature. He is remembered as a writer of brilliant irony and scepticism. France began his career as a poet and journalist and signed Zola's manifesto in support of Alfred Dreyfus, a Jewish army officer falsely convicted of espionage. He was an outspoken supporter of the 1917 Russian Revolution.

John Hope Franklin (1915–2009)

American historian of the United States, best known for his work *From Freedom to Slavery* (1947). Franklin was instrumental in developing the case that went on to make segregation in schools unconstitutional in 1954.

Sigmund Freud (1856–1939)

Austrian-Jewish neurologist and founder of psychoanalysis. He qualified as a doctor at the University of Vienna in 1881 but fled Austria in 1938 to escape Nazi persecution and died in exile in the UK. He is renowned for his theories on sexuality, dreams and the unconscious.

Robert Frost (1874–1963)

American poet who wrote about his native New England, through which he explored complex social and philosophical themes. He experienced grief throughout his life, losing his father, mother and wife before their time. He taught for forty years at the mountain campus of Ripton, Vermont.

Damon Galgut (b. 1963)

South African novelist and playwright who won the Booker Prize in 2021 for his novel *The Promise*. He claims the short story 'Pig' by Roald Dahl had the greatest influence on his writing. He writes with a fountain pen and refrains from using a computer until his third draft.

Mahatma Gandhi (1869–1948)

Indian lawyer, anti-colonial nationalist and political ethicist who employed non-violent resistance to lead the successful campaign for India's independence from British rule. He is a figurehead for civil rights and freedom across the world.

Martha Gellhorn (1908–98)

American novelist, travel writer and journalist, and one of the great war correspondents of the 20th century. She reported on virtually every major world conflict during her 60-year career. She was determined to become a journalist and worked at the United Press bureau in Paris but was fired after reporting sexual harassment by a colleague. She travelled Europe writing for newspapers and *Vogue*. In the 1930s, she helped Eleanor Roosevelt write correspondence, reported on the Great Depression and was fired for inciting workers to break their boss's office windows.

André Gide (1869–1951)

French author and winner of the Nobel Prize in Literature in 1947. Dubbed the greatest Frenchman of letters, Gide wrote fiction and autobiography, exploring the split between his Protestant upbringing and his homosexual adventurism.

John Gimlette (b. 1964)

English travel writer specialising in hot, humid, dangerous places who also holds down a career as a barrister in London. John travelled across the former Soviet Union at the age of 17 and has since been to over 60 countries.

Carlo Goldoni (1707–93)

Italian playwright and librettist from the Republic of Venice whose works include some of Italy's best-loved plays which dramatized the lives, values and conflicting interests of the emerging middle classes. His skill was in comedy, and he helped reform the Italian stage through his combination of wit and style in the vein of Molière.

Jason Goodwin (b. 1964)

English writer and historian who walked from Poland to Istanbul and wrote an account of his journey, *On Foot to the Golden Horn*, followed by a history of the Ottoman Empire, *Lords of the Horizons*.

His series of historical mystery novels feature Yashim, a eunuch detective, whose cookbook Jason has also written.

Maxim Gorky (1868–1936)

Russian writer with a long experience of exile and persecution for his radical politics, who worked by turns as dockworker, pedlar, tramp, garden-hand and scullery boy before succeeding as a writer. Known for his portrayal of people from the lower strata of society, he became very influential under Stalin.

Etienne de Grellet (1772–1855)

French-American Quaker missionary who fled France during the revolution and eventually settled in the US in 1795. Grellet carried out extensive mission work across North America, instigating educational policies in hospitals and prisons.

Ernesto Guevara (1928–67)

Ernesto 'Che' Guevara was an Argentine Marxist revolutionary, guerilla leader, military theorist and writer. A major figure of the Cuban revolution, his stylized visage has become a ubiquitous countercultural symbol of rebellion. As a young medical student he travelled throughout South America and became radicalized by the poverty, hunger and disease he witnessed, which empowered his desire to overturn the capitalist exploitation of Latin America by the US.

Woody Guthrie (1912–67)

One of the most significant figures in American folk music, his work focused on themes of American socialism and anti-fascism, penning songs such as 'This Land is your Land'. As a result of the dust storms in the 1930s, Woodie migrated from Oklahoma to California with thousands of other Okies. In LA he made friends with Steinbeck, played hillbilly music on KFVD station and wrote for a communist paper.

Jonas Hanway (Persian Hanway) (1712–86)

British philanthropist and traveller who, as a partner to Mr

Dingley, a merchant in St Petersburg, travelled through Russia and Persia. His first journey to Astrabad was impeded by sickness, attacks from pirates on the Caspian Sea and six weeks' quarantine. On return to London, his account of his travels soon made him a respected literary figure.

Augustus Hare (1834–1903)

English writer and raconteur who wrote memoirs, historical accounts and travel journals. He was a good friend of Somerset Maugham, who often visited him in Sussex.

John Hatt (b. 1948)

John Hatt spent a year in the City before working as a rep for Constable publishers. A year of travels in the Far East resulted in the *The Tropical Traveller: the essential guide to travel in hot countries.* In 1982 he set up Eland Publishing to republish the late, great Norman Lewis and after listening to an early devotee of the worldwide web on a long flight, he founded cheapflights.com in 1996 and sold it profitably ten years later.

Václav Havel (1936–2011)

Czech dissident, playwright and statesman, Havel first rose to prominence writing absurdist plays that criticized the Czechoslovak Socialist Republic. He set up several dissident initiatives and spent time in and out of prison. He was instrumental in the Velvet Revolution that toppled the communist government in 1989 and then served as the first democratically elected president of the country until its dissolution in 1992.

William Hazlitt (1778–1830)

English essayist, critic, painter and philosopher who, though little read and mostly out of print today, is considered one of the greatest critics and essayists in the English language.

Ernest Hemingway (1899–1961)

American writer known for his understated style which had a strong influence on 20th-century fiction. After sustaining a serious injury as an ambulance driver during WWI, he returned home but later moved to Paris where he fell under the influence of modernist writers and artists. He lived in London, France, Spain, Florida and finally Idaho, on a farmstead where he committed suicide in 1961.

Audrey Hepburn (1929–93)

Actress and humanitarian, recognised as both a film and fashion icon. Born in Brussels to an aristocratic family, she spent part of her childhood there and in England and the Netherlands. She studied ballet under Sonia Gaskell in Amsterdam and began performing in the chorus on West End productions in London, before starring in major movies.

Heraclitus (c.535–c.475 BCE)

Heraclitus of Ephesus was a pre-Socratic philosopher. Probably of privileged parentage, he later renounced his family wealth for the solitary life of a philosopher. He is remembered for his paradoxical thinking, appreciation of wordplay and a strong belief in the idea of 'flux' (the world in a constant state of change).

George Herbert (1593–1633)

Metaphysical poet, orator and parish priest, Herbert was considered a leading composer of devotional lyricism. He was known for his charitable nature, taking great care over his parishioners, particularly those in need. He died of consumption aged just 39.

Peter Hoeg (b. 1957)

Danish writer of fiction, best known for his novel *Miss Smila's Feeling for Snow* (1992). Born in Copenhagen, Denmark, he worked as a sailor, ballet dancer and actor before becoming a writer. His writing style has a reputation for being hard to place, incorporating postmodern, gothic and magical-realist elements.

Homer (b. 8th century BCE)

Ancient Greek author and epic poet, reputed author of *The Iliad* and *The Odyssey*, the foundational works of ancient Greek literature. Though little is known about his life, and even his status as the blind bard from Ionia is in doubt, the number of stories about him is testimony to his significance.

Horace (65–8 BCE)

Celebrated Latin satirical poet and witness to the changed nature of Rome as a capital city. Though patronised by the imperial court, he had fought on the Republican side in the civil war. His father was a freed slave who had risen to wealth and position through his own energy.

W H Hudson (1841–1922)

Anglo-Argentine author, naturalist and ornithologist who was born on a small estancia in Argentina. He spent his youth exploring the local flora and fauna. In 1874, he emigrated to England, married his landlady, the former singer Emily Wingrave, and supported himself as a writer.

Aldous Huxley (1894–1963)

English writer and philosopher who wrote nearly 50 books, as well as essays and poems. He lived in LA for the latter part of his life, and was considered one of the foremost intellectuals of his time. A pacifist, he was interested in philosophical mysticism and experimented with mescaline.

I Ching (c. 1000–750 BCE)

Usually translated as *The Book of Changes*, the *I Ching* is an ancient Chinese divination text and among the oldest of the Chinese classics. It played an influential role in Western understanding of East Asian philosophical thought. The 'changes' refer to the transformations of hexagrams, obtained when bunches of yarrow stalks are manipulated for purposes of divination.

Pico Iyer (b. 1957)

Siddharth Pico Raghavan Iyer is a British-born essayist, novelist and travel writer. The son of Indian academics, he started his career teaching writing and literature at Harvard University. In

1982 he joined *Time* as a writer on world affairs and has since travelled far and wide, from North Korea to Easter Island, writing fiction and non-fiction along the way.

Steve Jobs (1955-2011)

American entrepreneur and industrial designer who co-founded Apple and was a pioneer of the personal computer revolution of the 1970s and '80s. Born in San Francisco, he was adopted shortly after his birth. At school he fell in love with Shakespeare and electronics and began dabbling in drugs. He was an outsider, too clever for hipsters and too hispterish for academics. He dropped out of college and travelled to India in 1974, seeking enlightenment and studying Buddhism.

Samuel Johnson (1709–84)

English writer who made lasting contributions as a poet, playwright, essayist, moralist, critic and editor. In 1755 he compiled his famous *A Dictionary of the English Language*. Tall and large, he was described as having tics which would nowadays be diagnosed as Tourette's syndrome.

James Joyce (1882–1941)

Leading modernist writer who wrote with obsessive detail about his hometown of Dublin, yet lived in penury as an exile in Europe in order to escape the Catholic church's grip over the culture of Ireland. His two great works, *Ulysses* (1922) and *Finnegan's Wake* (1939) were only published after his health was already broken.

Juvenal (55–140 CE)

The satirical successor to the verse of Horace but from the perspective of an establishment lawyer, integrated within the imperial administration.

Dmetri Kakmi (b. 1961)

Turkish-born, Greek-Australian author who was born on the island of Bozcaada/Tenedos to Greek parents. His family migrated to Australia in 1971. He did not return to Tenedos until 1999. His memoir of growing up there, *Mother Land* (2008) was published to widespread acclaim. Until 2011, he worked as a senior editor at Penguin Books and he lives in Melbourne.

Santosh Kalwar (b. 1982)

A poet, writer and researcher who writes about truth, love and relationships. He is a self-published Nepalese writer and has published thirteen books as well as authoring newspaper columns and articles.

Jack Kerouac (1922–69)

American novelist and poet who, alongside Allen Ginsberg and William Burroughs, pioneered the Beat Generation. The publication of *On the Road* in 1957 earned him widespread fame and notoriety, setting off a cultural shock wave that inspired a generation to travel widely, meet new people and drink a lot. His writing influenced Bob Dylan, the Beatles and the Doors, among others.

Jean Kerr (1922–2003)

Irish-American author and playwright known for her humorous bestseller *Please Don't Eat the Daisies* and for her funny, sometimes cutting observations on American suburban life in the post-war era.

Michael Kerr (b. 1958)

Journalist who worked for 27 years at the *Daily Telegraph*, before leaving to spend more time writing, travelling and editing deskboundtraveller.com.

Rudyard Kipling (1865–1935)

English journalist, short-story writer, poet and novelist, Kipling was born in British India which inspired much of his writing. He is best known for his children's works, especially *The Jungle Book*.

Charles Kuralt (1934–97)

American journalist known for his long career at CBS and for his 'On the Road' segments for the evening news. Kuralt hired a motor home and drove along the back roads of America, avoiding interstates to get to the heart of the nation and its people.

Louis L'Amour (1908–88)

An American novelist and short-story writer famous for his Frontier stories. His writing was inspired by his upbringing in farm country and later on, after his father went bankrupt, by his family's itinerant, hard lifestyle on the road.

Alfonse de Lamartine (1790–1869)

French author, poet and statesman. Born into provincial nobility, he first rose to fame as a poet. In politics he championed democratic ideals and helped abolish slavery and the death penalty.

Lao Tzu (6th–4th century BCE)

A semi-legendary figure, Lao is the founder of Taoist philosophy and a contemporary of Confucius. His work has been embraced by anti-authoritarian movements throughout history. It is said that he grew weary of the moral decay in his homeland and ventured west as a hermit. On reaching the frontier, a guard asked him to record his wisdom before passing through. The guard was so touched by the work, he left his post and followed Lao.

T E Lawrence (1888–1935)

British archaeologist, army officer and writer known for his role in the Arab Revolt and the Sinai and Palestine Campaign (1915–18) against the Ottoman Empire during the First World War. Nicknamed Lawrence of Arabia, the title was used for the 1962 film based on his wartime activities. He died in a motorcycle accident after swerving to avoid two children on their bicycles in Dorset.

Ursula K Le Guin (1929–2018)

American author best known for her works in speculative fiction and her creation of the Hainish universe. In a career spanning sixty years, she produced more than twenty novels and over a hundred short-stories. She became the first woman to win both the Hugo and Nebula awards for best novel.

Paddy Leigh Fermor (1915–2011)
English writer, scholar and soldier who served behind the lines in the Cretan resistance in World War II. Widely seen as Britain's greatest travel writer, he was described by a BBC journalist as 'a cross between Indiana Jones, James Bond and Graham Greene'. At 18 he walked the length of Europe with a book of verse and a few clothes, sleeping in monasteries, barges and country houses along the way.

Doris Lessing (1919–2013)
British-Zimbabwean novelist who became the oldest person ever to receive the Nobel Prize in Literature in 2007. Her Nobel acceptance speech cited fiction writers as having the power to redress inequalities, saying 'it is our imaginations which shape us, keep us, create us – for good and for ill.'

Claude Lévi-Strauss (1908–2009)
French anthropologist and ethnologist who grew up in Paris, joined the political left and excelled in academia before moving to Brazil to carry out ethnographic fieldwork. His famous book, *Tristes Tropiques* (1955), outlined his structuralist belief in the universal nature of human characteristics, that there is no structural difference between a 'savage' and a 'civilized' mind.

Norman Lewis (1908–2003)
Influential British writer, best known for his travel writing, especially *Naples '44* and *A Dragon Apparent*. His article 'Genocide in Brazil' led to the creation of Survival International, an organisation dedicated to the protection of first peoples around the world.

David Livingstone (1813–73)
Scottish physician, pioneer Christian missionary and explorer in Africa who believed that if he could find the sources of the Nile, he would have enough influence to end the East African Arab-Swahili slave trade. His exploration of central Africa

ended in his disappearance and death, leaving in his wake missionary initiatives that would lead the 'Scramble for Africa'.

Henry Wadsworth Longfellow (1807–82)

American poet and educator whose lyrical poetry, known for its musicality, includes 'The Song of Hiawatha'. The most popular American poet of his day, he has been criticised for being too sentimental.

Federico García Lorca (1898–1936)

Spanish poet, playwright and theatre director who achieved international recognition as a major poet who introduced European tenets and movements into Spanish poetry. He was murdered by Nationalist forces at the beginning of the Spanish Civil War and his remains have never been found.

Amin Maalouf (b. 1949)

Lebanese-born French author who has written award-winning fiction and non-fiction in French, his second language. He worked as a director of a Beirut newspaper before the civil war broke out in 1975, when he moved to Paris.

Shirley MacLaine (b. 1934)

American actress known for her portrayals of eccentric, strong-willed women. MacLaine has won numerous awards over a seven-decade career, has an unusual interest in UFOs and has written books on spirituality and transcendental meditation.

Ella Maillart (1903–97)

Swiss adventurer, travel writer, photographer and sportswoman, Ella sailed around the Mediterranean at the age of 20, before competing in the 1924 Summer Olympics. From the 1930s onwards she explored the Muslim republics of the Soviet Union and other parts of Asia, writing about and photographing her travels in books like *Forbidden Journey*, which chronicled the journey she made with Peter Fleming.

Beryl Markham (1902–86)

An English-born Kenyan aviator, Markham was the first person to fly solo, non-stop, across the Atlantic from Britain to North America. After years of obscurity, her memoir *West with the Night* (1942) was rediscovered by Hemingway who described the book as 'bloody wonderful'. She was living in poverty at the time, in a house outside of Nairobi. The proceeds from the reprint allowed her to finish her life in relative comfort.

Justin Marozzi (b. 1970)

English journalist, historian and travel writer whose first book, *South from Barbary*, described an adventurous journey across southern Libya by camel. He has subsequently written biographies and narrative history.

Elizabeth Marshall Thomas (b. 1931)

Elizabeth Marshall Thomas credits her parents with developing her observational skills. From a very young age, her father would take her to watch wildlife. Later, the entire family went to live with the Bushmen of the Kalahari Desert, with her mother, Lorna Marshall, 'one of the most sensitive, meticulous and unpretentious ethnographers of all time'. This experience led Elizabeth to write *The Harmless People* about the Bushmen, though she is now best known for her work on the lives of dogs and wolves.

Steve Martin (b. 1945)

American actor, comedian, writer, producer and musician who first came to notice as a writer for *The Smothers Brothers Comedy Hour* in the 1960s. After starring in blockbuster films throughout the '80s and '90s, he dedicated himself to playing the banjo in bluegrass groups. He was awarded a Grammy for his first solo album. He had considered becoming a professor of philosophy, but instead logic and non-sequiturs influenced his comedy.

Andrew Marvell (1621–78)

Metaphysical poet, satirist and politician, a colleague and friend of John Milton during the Commonwealth. From 1642 onwards, he travelled in Europe, mastering four languages. After the Restoration, Marvell avoided punishment for his co-operation with republicanism and helped convince Charles II's government to not execute John Milton for his antimonarchical writings.

Guy De Maupassant (1850–93)

French writer, born and raised within the provincial society of Normandy, who brilliantly observed the reality of bourgeois France after the Industrial Revolution. Friend of Flaubert and Zola, the author of 300 short stories and the cynical, wicked but immortal, *Bel Ami* (1885).

Frances Mayes (b. 1940)

American novelist whose memoir *Under the Tuscan Sun* (1996) was on the New York Times bestseller list for over two years and was adapted to film. The book is about Mayes' experiences renovating an abandoned villa in rural Cortona. She has published several poetry collections and was editor of *The Best American Travel Writing 2002*.

Robin McKinley (b. 1952)

American author of fantasy and children's books. Much of her writing is inspired by classic fairytale narratives to which she puts her own feminist twist. Her books feature strong female leads who don't need rescuing but instead shape events themselves.

Margaret Mead (1901–78)

American cultural anthropologist. Considered controversial as an academic, Mead's research into attitudes around sex in South Pacific and South Asian cultures influenced the sexual revolution of the 1960s. Her studies were concerned with the problems of child rearing, personality and culture and how ethical standards differ from place to place.

Herman Melville (1819–91)

American writer best remembered for *Moby Dick* (1851), considered one of the great American novels. He took to the sea as a common sailor in 1839, and his adventures after jumping ship at the Marquesas Islands were the basis for his first two books.

James Michener (1907–97)

American writer of more than 40 books, most of which were long, fictional family sagas covering the lives of many generations in specific locations, such as Hawaii. Michener never met his biological parents and was raised a Quaker by an adoptive mother in Pennsylvania. His breakout work, *Tales of the South Pacific*, was inspired by his experiences in the US Navy during World War II.

Henry Miller (1891–1980)

American novelist who broke existing literary forms and developed a new type of semi-autobiographical novel. All of his books, based on experiences in New York and Paris, were banned in the US until 1961. During his time in Paris, he was influenced by the Surrealists.

Michel de Montaigne (1533–92)

One of the most significant philosophers of the French renaissance, Montaigne is known for making the essay a literary genre, merging anecdotes and autobiography to reach intellectual conclusions. In his lifetime, Montaigne was admired more as a statesman than as an author. Admired later for his free embrace of doubt and uncertainty, he coined the famous phrase '*Que sais-je?*' – 'What do I know?'

Montesquieu (1689–1755)

French man of letters, historian and political philosopher, he was a key figure of the enlightenment who worked towards reform of the despotism of the French monarchy. He argued for a separation and a balance of powers, and a system of 'government that should be set up so that no man need be afraid of another'. His *Persian Letters*, a satirical survey of France by two foreign travellers, made his name when published in 1721 but *The Spirit of the* Law, which proved incredibly influential to the leaders of the American War of Independence, had to be printed privately.

George Moore (1852–1933)

Irish writer who was influenced by Zola, drawing on French realism in his naturalistic writings, and who in turn influenced James Joyce. His novels were controversial for their detailed accounts of love affairs.

Jan Morris (1926–2020)

Foreign correspondent, free spirit and writer, best known for her *Pax Britannica* trilogy, a history of the British empire. Morris wrote for *The Times*, famously catching the worldwide scoop of the first ascent of Everest by Edmund Hillary and Tenzing Norgay. Morris is most admired for her free-standing essays, as well as for the complete candour with which she wrote about her gender-reassignment surgery in *Conundrum*.

Fynes Moryson (1566–1630)

A traveller who journeyed through Europe and the Eastern Mediterranean, writing about it in his multi-volume *Itinerary*. His work is of great value to historians for its depiction of the social conditions in the lands he visited. The son of a Lincolnshire gentleman, his antipathy to Irish priests and Turks makes him an unreliable source for analysing their cultures.

The Prophet Muhammad (570–632)

Religious, social and political leader of the Arabs and the founder of Islam. Muhammed continued in the tradition of Abraham, Moses, Jesus and the old prophets but with a new urgency in a series of 114 divine revelations (*The Koran*) that were delivered in Arabic over the last twenty-two years of his life.

John Muir (1838–1914)

Influential Scottish-American naturalist, author and early advocate for preserving the wilderness in America, who helped preserve the Yosemite Valley and Sequoia National Park through his activism. In 1867 he walked from Kentucky to Florida, a journey recounted in *A Thousand Mile Walk*.

Fitzhugh Mullan (1942–2019)

American physician, writer, educator and social activist whose activism started in the 1960s when he spent time in Mississippi as a civil rights worker. He led the Gates Foundation-funded Sub-Saharan African Medical Schools Study.

Haruki Murakami (b. 1949)

Japanese writer who published his first novel while working in his own small jazz bar. He is known for his magic realism, spanning genres from science fiction and crime fiction to fantasy. He has divided literary critics in Japan for being un-Japanese, although internationally he is considered one of the greatest living novelists.

Iris Murdoch (1919–99)

Irish-British novelist and philosopher best known for her novels about good and evil, sexual relationships and morality. She worked for HM Treasury before studying philosophy as a postgraduate at Cambridge. She was refused a visa to enter the US on account of being a member of the Communist Party of Great Britain.

Dervla Murphy (1931–2022)

Irish travel writer and international activist, best known for her 1965 book *Full Tilt*, in which she recounts her overland cycling trip through Europe, Iran, Afghanistan, Pakistan and India. Murphy travelled far and wide either alone or with family and avoided luxuries, depending on the hospitality of local people. She wrote 26 books about her travels.

Bill Murray (b. 1950)

American actor and comedian known for his deadpan delivery. He rose to fame on *The National Lampoon Radio Hour* in the '70s, before appearing on *Saturday Night Live*. He won a Golden Globe for his role in *Lost in Translation*.

Thomas Nashe (1567–1601)

Elizabethan playwright, poet and satirist who fled Cambridge in the middle of his bachelor's degree, supposedly to avoid expulsion after appearing in a raucous play. He moved to London where he began his literary career, but was still regularly caught up in controversies.

Jawaharlal Nehru (1889–1964)

Indian anti-colonial nationalist, secular humanist and author who was a central figure in India in the middle of the 20th century. Nehru served as Prime Minister for 17 years after independence, promoting parliamentary democracy, secularism and technology during the '50s, influencing India's arc as a modern nation. He has been hailed as the 'architect of Modern India' and praised for preventing ethnic civil war.

John Julius Norwich (1929–2018)

English historian, travel writer and television personality, his father was a Conservative politician and his mother a famous beauty and society figure. While in the British Foreign Service, he served in Yugoslavia and Lebanon but resigned to become a writer after his father's death.

George Orwell (1903–50)

Eric Arthur Blair, known by his pen name George Orwell, was an English novelist, essayist and journalist famed for his lucid prose, opposition to totalitarianism and support of socialism. His works include the allegorical novella *Animal Farm* and the dystopian novel *Nineteen Eighty-Four*. The term 'Orwellian' is now part of the English language and refers to totalitarian social practices.

Ovid (43 BCE–17 CE)

Urbane, literate establishment poet chronicling his lust for life and how best to make love, both for humankind and the gods. *Amores, Ars Armatoria* and *Metamorphoses* have been read for two thousand years, but their hedonistic amorality infuriated Emperor Augustus who exiled Ovid to the Black Sea.

Michael Palin (b. 1943)

An English actor and comedian who rose to fame as part of Monty Python, an iconic British comedy group. Later Michael took to travel writing and documentary film making for the BBC, journeying all over the world.

Paracelsus (1993–1541)

Swiss physician, alchemist and philosopher who pioneered toxicology. He was influential as a prophet, as well, combining observation with received wisdom. He travelled across Europe as a young man, in pursuit of universal knowledge.

Dorothy Parker (1893–1967)

American poet, writer, critic and satirist who was known for her wit and eye for 20th-century urban foibles. She had a troubled childhood, rising to fame for works published in the *New Yorker* and as a founding member of the Algonquin Round Table. She was placed on the Hollywood blacklist for her involvement in left-wing politics, which curtailed her screenwriting career.

Pascal (1632–62)

Blaise Pascal was a French mathematician, physicist, inventor, philosopher, writer and theologian. A child prodigy, he was educated by his father and wrote a significant treatise on projective geometry at the age of 16. Soon afterwards he corresponded with Pierre de Fermat on probability theory, which informs modern economics to this day.

Cesare Pavese (1908–50)

An Italian writer and translator of English literature, in 1935 he was arrested for possession of letters from an anti-fascist political prisoner. After internal exile in Southern Italy, he returned to Turin to work for a left-wing publisher. He killed himself in 1950.

John Pendlebury (1904–41)

British archaeologist who worked for British intelligence during World War II. Born in London, he lost an eye at the age of two, an injury that would fuel his desire to outperform others later on in life. After leaving Cambridge he went to Athens to study Egyptian artefacts found in Greece. He was captured and executed by German troops during the battle for Crete.

Pericles (495–429 BCE)

Greek politician during the Golden Age of Athens. His mother supposedly had a vision of carrying a lion in her womb before his birth. He turned the Delian league into the Athenian empire and promoted arts and literature, helping Athens to acquire its reputation as the cultural centre of the ancient Greek world.

Pliny (23–79CE)

Pliny the Elder was a Roman author, naturalist and naval commander whose *Naturalis Historia* was a precursor to modern encyclopaedias. He died in AD 79, attempting to rescue a friend and his family by ship during the eruption of Mount Vesuvius. The wind from the eruption would not allow his ship to leave port.

Alexander Pope (1688–1744)

English poet, translator and satirist widely considered the foremost poet of the early 18th century. His poetry is best known for its satirical and discursive elements (*The Rape of the Lock* and *The Dunciad*). He also translated the works of Homer.

Dennis Potter (1935–94)

English television dramatist, screenwriter and journalist best known for his BBC television series *Pennies from Heaven* (1978) and *The Singing Detective* (1986). His work mixed fantasy and reality and dealt with issues of social mobility as well as themes from popular culture.

Matthew Prior (1664–1721)

English poet and diplomat. Prior was a precocious student, translating Horace at twelve and having his education funded by an impressed Lord Dorset. He rose to fame as a satirist and gained patronage and promotion along the way, holding prestigious diplomatic positions in Holland and France.

V S Pritchett (1900–97)

British writer and literary critic best known for his short stories. Victor left school at 16 to work as a leather buyer, before moving to Paris as a shop assistant. In 1923 he started writing for the *Christian Science Monitor*, which sent him to Ireland and Spain, journeys which he wrote about in his first two books.

Sextus Propertius (48–15 BCE)

Latin elegiac poet whose memory is kept alive by just one surviving book, dedicated to his mistress Cynthia.

Marcel Proust (1871–1922)

Proust wrote the monumental novel *In Search of Lost Time*, one of the most influential works of the 20th century. He drew on childhood memories in his writing, recalling the atmosphere of a declining aristocracy and rising middle class. Among his peers, he was known for his hypersexuality, dilettantism and close relationship with his mother.

Jonathan Raban (b. 1942)

British travel writer, critic and novelist whose most celebrated works include *Old Glory*, *Coasting*, *Hunting Mr Heartbreak* and *Badlands*. Since 1990, Raban has lived in Seattle.

Arthur Rimbaud (1854–91)

French poet known for his transgressive and surreal themes and for his influence on modern literature and arts. He started writing at a very young age, abandoned his education in his teens, ran away to Paris and wrote his last major work by the age of 20 – *Illuminations*. He was a libertine and restless soul, engaged in a fiery romantic relationship with fellow poet Paul Verlaine. After retiring from writing, he travelled three continents as a merchant and explorer until his early death from cancer.

Barnaby Rogerson (b. 1960)

Rogerson has written a biography of the Prophet Muhammad, *A History of North Africa*, *The Heirs of the Prophet Muhammad* and *The House Divided: Sunni and Shia conflicts in the Middle East*. In 2000 he bought Eland Publishing from John Hatt.

Henry Rollins (b. 1961)

American musician, writer, spoken word artist, actor and presenter who started out as a punk rocker, moved into spoken word and has been a strong campaigner for LGBT rights and World Hunger Relief.

John Ruskin (1819–1900)

English writer, philosopher, art critic and polymath of the Victorian era. He wrote on a variety of subjects – geology, architecture, myth, ornithology, botany and literature – but is best known for his work on art. His writing emphasised the connection between nature, art and society, anticipating recent interest in environmentalism, sustainability and craft.

Moslih Eddin Saadi (1210–91)

Known by his pen name Saadi, he was the major Persian poet and prose writer of the medieval period. Widely recognized as the greatest poets of the classical literary tradition, Saadi has the epithet 'The Wordsmith'. Born a Sunni Muslim in Shiraz, the Mongol invasions of Iran forced him to lead an itinerant life.

Saki (1870–1916)

The pen name of Hector Hugh Munro, a British writer whose witty and sometimes macabre stories satirized Edwardian society. A master of the short story, he started out writing sketches for newspapers lampooning political figures of the day. Following the downfall of Oscar Wilde, he kept his sexuality a secret. Despite being too old to join the army, he insisted on serving in the ranks and was killed by a German sniper at the age of 43.

J D Salinger (1919–2010)

American author best known for his 1951 novel *The Catcher in the Rye*. Its depiction of adolescent alienation and loss of innocence in the protagonist Holden Caulfield has been hugely influential in popular culture.

George Sand (1804–76)

One of the most popular writers in Europe in her lifetime, Amantine Lucile Aurore Dupin was a French writer known by the pen name George Sand. She wore male attire in public, both for practical reasons and to subvert stereotypes. She gained access to venues barred to women and smoked tobacco in public. She had numerous intense love affairs, including one with Chopin whilst he was convalescing on Mallorca.

Jean-Paul Sartre (1905–80)

French philosopher, writer, proponent of atheist existentialism and radical activist. Sartre fought in the French army, served in the Resistance to Nazi occupation, supported the 1968 student rebellion and opposed American involvement in Vietnam.

Anthony Sattin (b. 1956)

British journalist, broadcaster and writer of several acclaimed books of history and travel: *The Pharaohs Shadow: travels in Ancient and Modern Egypt*, *The Gates of Africa*, *A Winter on the Nile: Florence Nightingale, Gustave Flaubert and the Temptations of Egypt*, followed by *Young Lawrence: a Portrait of the Legend as a Young Man*, and most recently *Nomads*.

Chief Seattle (1786–1866)

A Squamish and Duwamish chief who formed a personal

relationship with leading white settlers in his native northeast. The city of Seattle, in Washington, is named after him. He earned a reputation from an early age as a leader and a warrior. A famous speech, pleading for respect for the rights of Native Americans and for environmental values, has been attributed to him.

David Sedaris (b. 1956)

American humourist, comedian and author who first came to attention when his essay *Santaland Diaries* was broadcast on National Public Radio in 1992. His humour is self-deprecating and draws on his own experiences growing up in the middle-class suburbs of Raleigh, North Carolina.

Seneca (4 BCE–65 CE)

Roman stoic philosopher, statesman and dramatist. In 41 CE, he was exiled to Corsica under Emperor Claudius, but returned in 49 to become a tutor to Nero. He was forced to take his life in 65 for alleged complicity in the Pisonian conspiracy to assassinate Nero, of which he is likely to have been innocent. His plays were all tragedies and were venerated in the Renaissance.

Anita Septimus

American social worker and psychotherapist, who has worked with young children with AIDS.

Dr Seuss (1904–91)

Pen name of Theodor Seuss Geisel, an American children's author, political cartoonist, illustrator, poet and animator. His work includes many of the most popular children's books of all time, selling over 600 million copies and translated into 20 languages by the time of his death.

Tahir Shah (b. 1966)

British author, journalist and documentary maker of Afghan-Indian descent. Both his grandfathers were respected literary figures and his father – the writer, Idries Shah – was friends with Doris Lessing, J D Salinger and Robert Graves. This had a profound effect on Tahir's education. Despite his dyslexia, he became a successful writer.

William Shakespeare (1564–1616)

English playwright, poet and actor widely regarded as the greatest writer in the English language and the world's greatest dramatist. From Stratford-upon-Avon, he moved to London sometime between 1585 and 1592 where he began a successful career as an actor, writer and part-owner of a theatre company, the Lord Chamberlain's Men.

George Bernard Shaw (1856–1950)

Irish playwright, critic, polemicist and political activist who wrote more than sixty plays, including *Man and Superman* (1902), *Pygmalion* (1913) and *Saint Joan* (1923). He was a member of the Fabian Society, inspired greatly by the writings of Karl Marx. His views were often contentious; promoting eugenics and opposing vaccinations.

John A Shedd (1859–1928)

John Augustus Shedd was an American teacher who developed Shedd's Natural Memory Method, a way of using mnemonics as a memory technique, backed by two self-improving books: *Improvement of the Memory* and *A Perfect Memory: How to Attain It*. Right at the end of his life, he put together a collection of moral adages called *Salt from My Attic*.

Percy Bysshe Shelley (1792–1822)

One of the major English Romantic poets, Shelley did not achieve fame in his lifetime but would later gain popularity among poets, as well as radical political thinkers such as Marx, Gandhi and Bernard Shaw. His life was marked by family crises, ill health and a backlash against his atheism. In 1818 he went into permanent self-exile in Italy, eloping with Mary Shelley, author of *Frankenstein*. He died in a boating accident aged 29.

Rupert Smith (b. 1960)

Onetime barman and restaurateur, traveller in Hellenic lands, teacher of the classics and freelance lecturer, currently living between the island of Syros and the city of Bath.

Spinoza (1632–77)

Baruch de Spinoza was a Dutch philosopher of Portuguese Sephardic Jewish origin. Inspired by Descartes, he was one of the seminal thinkers of the Enlightenment, shunned by Jewish society in Amsterdam after voicing controversial ideas regarding the authenticity of the Hebrew Bible when he was 23. He led a simple life and worked as an optical lens grinder.

Charles Spurgeon (1834–92)

English Baptist preacher and influential Christian figure said to give sermons at the Metropolitan Tabernacle in London to spellbound crowds.

St Augustine (354–430)

A roman citizen of North Africa who became a Manichean follower ('hearer') while studying in Carthage. He later rose through the ranks of the infant Roman Catholic church, at one and the same time a compassionate, hard-working parish priest and a vicious intellectual attack dog. His letters, sermons and autobiography remain inspirational.

Freya Stark (1893–1993)

British explorer and travel writer who wrote more than two dozen books on her travels through the Middle East. Growing up in Italy, Stark suffered an unfortunate accident which left her face disfigured. She was brave, industrious, self-willed and a fluent conversationist. During the Second World War she disseminated pro-British propaganda across the Arab world.

John Steinbeck (1902–68)

One of the most famous and widely read American writers of the 20th century, his works mainly examine the lives of the working class and migrant workers during the Great Depression. During this period, he and his wife Carol lived in a cottage in Monterey, surviving on fish from the sea and vegetables from their garden.

Adlai Stevenson I (1835–1914)

American politician who served as 23rd Vice President of the US from 1893–97.

Robert Louis Stevenson (1850–94)

Scottish writer best known for works such as *Treasure Island* and *The Strange Case of Dr Jekyll and Mr Hyde*. His father's family were famous engineers, although his travels with his father to the Orkney and Shetland Islands' lighthouses they had built inspired his writing more than his interest in engineering. He suffered from bronchial trouble for much of his life, but travelled widely nonetheless.

Harry Caskie Stinnett (1911–98)

American travel writer whose stories and essays appeared in various magazines and periodicals. He owned a three-and-half-acre island called 'Hamloaf' in Maine and appreciated the island for 'looking the same as it did 1,000 years ago'.

Tom Stoppard (b. 1937)

Czech-born British playwright and screenwriter known for dealing with human rights, censorship and political freedom in his plays. He is one of the most internationally performed dramatists of his generation. He fled Czechoslovakia as a Jewish child refugee when Nazi invasion was imminent.

Sophie Swetchine (1782–1857)

Known as Madame Swetchine, the Russian mystic was famed for her salon in Paris. Born in Moscow, she spent her early years at the court of Catherine the Great as her father was one of the empress's closest advisors. She was forced into exile after converting to Catholicism.

Frank Tatchell (early 20th century)

Anglican clergyman and a lifelong enthusiast for the simple charms of walking and foreign travel. His advice, some of it useful, some of it almost wilfully eccentric, is also touched by the example of Christ. *The Happy Traveller: A Book for Poor Men*, was first published in 1923.

Matthew Teller (b. 1969)

A family holiday to Jerusalem when he was 11 ignited Matthew Teller's love for travelling and for exploring unfamiliar regions. He produces documentaries for BBC radio, writes guidebooks and books about the Middle East.

Paul Theroux (b. 1941)

American novelist and travel writer who has written numerous books, including *The Great Railway Bazaar* (1975). Theroux went to the University of Maine before joining the Peace Corps in 1963 as a teacher in Malawi. He has criticized celebrities over the years for creating the impression that Africa is troubled and can only be saved by outside help.

Wilfred Thesiger (1910–2003)

Thesiger was a British explorer, military officer and writer, best known for *Arabian Sands* (1959), his account of crossing the Empty Quarter of the Arabian Peninsula by foot and camel. Born in Ethiopia to a British Consul-General father, he never forgot the colour and variety of local customs he saw there as a child, and after studying in England, he returned to Africa.

Hugh Thomson (b.1960)

A writer, documentary film maker and explorer, Hugh's books on South America include *The White Rock: an exploration of the Inca heartland*, *Cochineal Red: travels through ancient Peru* and *Tequila Oil: getting lost in Mexico*.

Joseph Thomson (1858–95)

British geologist and explorer who played a major part in the

Scramble for Africa. He excelled more as an explorer than as a scientist. A gazelle and a waterfall are named after him. He avoided confrontations, going by the motto, 'He who goes gently, goes safely; he who goes safely, goes far.'

Henry David Thoreau (1817–62)

American naturalist, essayist, poet and philosopher known for his pioneering role in transcendentalism. His most famous book *Walden* records his experience leading a simple life in the countryside. His philosophy is considered a precursor to modern-day environmentalism.

Colin Thubron (b. 1939)

British travel writer and novelist who worked in publishing in England and New York before making independent documentary films for the BBC. He has written travel books on the Middle East, Russia and the Far East, as well as novels set (unlike his travel writing) in enclosed spaces, such as prisons, palaces and hospitals.

Alice B Toklas (1877–1967)

Lover and co-saloniste with Gertrude Stein in Paris, Toklas was Jewish-American and moved to Paris after the San Francisco earthquake in 1906. She met Stein the day after she arrived, and they were together until the latter's death in 1946. Stein's most famous book was *The Autobiography of Alice B Toklas*.

Leo Tolstoy (1828–1910)

Russian writer, mystic and finally philosopher of a non-violent, simple peasant life. Tolstoy started as a dissolute aristocrat, with periods of military service and supervising his estates. *War and Peace* (the world's favourite novel) was started when he became a father and was succeeded by *Anna Karenina*. By 1901 his political philosophy, which verged on a cult, encouraged the Orthodox Church to formally excommunicate him.

George Trevelyan (1838–1928)
British statesman and author who worked as a civil servant in India from 1862. His experiences led to his writing *Cawnpore*, an account of the massacre there during the Indian rebellion of 1857. He was a member of the Liberal party and famously fell out with Gladstone over the 1886 Irish Home Rule Bill.

Mark Twain (1835–1910)
American writer most famous for *The Adventures of Tom Sawyer* and *The Adventures of Huckleberry Finn*. From Missouri, Twain worked as a typesetter, a riverboat pilot and a miner before moving into journalism.

Anne Tyler (b. 1941)
American writer often likened to John Updike, Jane Austen and Eudora Welty. Born in Minnesota to Quaker parents, she grew up in a Quaker commune in the mountains of North Carolina. By the time she was eleven she had never attended public school nor used a telephone, which allowed her to view the normal world with surprise.

Vincent Van Gogh (1853–90)
Dutch post-impressionist painter who posthumously became one of the most famous figures in Western art. Over one decade he produced 2,100 artworks of landscapes, self-portraits and still lifes characterised by bold colours and expressive brushwork. He severed his own left ear with a razor after a confrontation with his friend Gauguin and spent time in a psychiatric hospital in Paris. He committed suicide at 37 and has become the prototype of the misunderstood genius, the tortured artist.

Virgil (70–19 BCE)
The most celebrated of all the Latin poets, he stands just beneath Homer in the pantheon of classical writers. His talent was nursed by the patronage of the imperial court, which was rewarded

by *The Georgics*, *The Eclogues* and *The Aeneid*, upon which he worked for the last eleven years of his life.

Derek Walcott (1930–2017)

Saint Lucian poet and playwright who received the 1992 Nobel Prize in Literature. His family is of English, Dutch and African descent, reflecting the complex colonial history of the island that he explores in his poetry. Walcott published his first poem when he was 14.

Irving Wallace (1916–90)

American bestselling author and screenwriter known for his heavily researched novels with sexual themes. Born into a Jewish family of Russian descent, Wallace began selling stories to magazines as a teenager.

Orson Welles (1915–85)

American director, actor, screenwriter and producer, considered one of the most influential filmmakers of all time. His Halloween radio adaptation of *The War of the Worlds* caused some listeners to believe an actual invasion by extra-terrestrial beings was occurring. Born in Wisconsin, he was institutionalised for learning difficulties as a child. A lifelong magician and singer, he performed extensively and presented troop variety shows during the war years.

Mae West (1893–1980)

American actress known for her breezy sexual independence. She was active in vaudeville and on stage in New York before moving to LA to work in film. One of the most controversial stars of her day, she was often censored which, she quipped, made her a 'fortune'. Her first starring role on Broadway was in a 1926 play she wrote called *Sex*, for which she was prosecuted on morals charges.

Sara Wheeler (b. 1961)

Prominent female travel writer best known for her explorations of the polar regions, which resulted in *Terra Incognita: Travels* in Antarctica, *Cherry: A life of Apsley Cherry-Garrard*, and *The Magnetic North: Travels in the Arctic*. She has recently been commissioned to write the biography of Jan Morris.

James Whitfield (1822–71)

African-American poet, abolitionist and political activist whose parents both died by the time he was seven. In 1839 he was working as a barber in upstate New York, whilst writing in his free time. His poem *America* gained attention for its take on the hypocrisy of a supposedly free, democratic America.

Walt Whitman (1819–92)

American poet, essayist and journalist, among the most influential poets in the American canon. He was scrutinised during his life for his overtly sensual lyrics and his homosexuality. After working for years in low level jobs, he self-published *Leaves of Grass* anonymously. The book quickly became a sensation and was endorsed by Ralph Waldo Emerson.

Oscar Wilde (1854–1900)

Irish poet and playwright who became one of the most popular playwrights in London in the early 1890s. He is also remembered for his novel *The Picture of Dorian Gray* and for his criminal conviction for homosexuality.

Isambard Wilkinson (b. 1971)

Wilkinson has worked as a foreign correspondent for the *Daily Telegraph* and the *Economist* in Pakistan and Spain, and on assignment in other countries including Algeria, Palestine, Israel, Iraq, Zimbabwe and Afghanistan. His travels abroad have been interrupted twice by kidney failure, enabling him to take time off to recuperate with his grandmother in the Irish countryside, which is home.

Tennessee Williams (1911–83)

Pen name of Thomas Lanier Williams III, one of the foremost playwrights of 20th-century America. His father, a travelling shoe salesman, became an alcoholic and though his mother protected him from his father's violent outbursts, Williams drew on his dysfunctional family in much of his writing. He was 33 when he first received attention for his play *The Glass Menagerie* (1944), after years of struggling to make it as a writer.

Jasper Winn (b. 1959)

Jasper writes about slow adventures based on kayaking, walking, cycling, sailing and horse riding. He currently lives off-grid on a 27ft sailing boat and has previously published *Paddle*, about kayaking around Ireland and *Water Ways* about the history of Britain's canals and the lives of contemporary inland boaters.

George Winters

George Winters was born in Eldon, Missouri and was in the Army during the Vietnam War.

Thomas Wolfe (1900–38)

American novelist known for his lengthy novels, mixing rhapsodic, poetic prose with autobiographical writing. Born in North Carolina and the youngest of eight children, Wolfe's father used an angel in his shop window to attract customers, a figure that would feature greatly in his son's writing.

Virginia Woolf (1882–1941)

One of the most important English modernist authors and a pioneer in the use of stream of consciousness as a narrative device. Encouraged by her father to write, she moved from her affluent home in South Kensington to bohemian Bloomsbury, where she and her brothers' intellectual friends formed the Bloomsbury Group. Though married to Leonard Woolf, she also had romantic relationships with women, including Vita Sackville-West, who inspired her writing greatly. Throughout her life, she was troubled by mental illness and drowned herself in the River Ouse in Sussex aged 59.

William Wordsworth (1770–1850)

English Romantic poet whose *magnum opus* was the semi-autobiographical poem of his early years, *The Prelude*, though he is probably best known for his poem extolling the pleasures of daffodils. Wordsworth had a distant father and often lived with his maternal grandparents in Penrith.

Antony Wynn (b. 1949)

Antony Wynn read Persian and Turkish at Balliol and went on to live in Iran, first buying carpets and then running a racecourse. His books include *Persia in the Great Game*, and *Three Camels to Smyrna*.

W B Yeats (1865–1939)

Irish poet, dramatist and writer who was one of the foremost figures in 20th-century literature. A Protestant of Anglo-Irish descent, he was greatly inspired by Irish legends and folklore. He fell in love with Maud Gonne, an ardent Irish nationalist, but was rejected by her on several occasions. His unhappy love life made its way into a number of his poems.

Lin Yutang (1895–1976)

Chinese inventor, linguist, novelist, philosopher and translator who translated classic Chinese texts into English. His informal but polished style in both Chinese and English made him one of the most influential writers of his generation. From 1923–26 he taught English at Peking University, introducing humour, a Western concept, to Chinese readers.

ELAND

61 Exmouth Market, London EC1R 4QL
Email: info@travelbooks.co.uk

Eland was started in 1982 to revive great travel books which had fallen out of print. Although the list soon diversified into biography and fiction, all the titles are chosen for their interest in spirit of place. One of our readers explained that for him reading an Eland is like listening to an experienced anthropologist at the bar – she's let her hair down and is telling all the stories that were just too good to go into the textbook.

Eland books are for travellers, and for those who are content to travel in their own minds. We can never quite define what we are looking for, but they need to be observant of others, to catch the moment and place on the wing and to have a page-turning gift for storytelling. And they might do that while being, by turns, funny, wry, intelligent, humane, universal, self-deprecating and idiosyncratic. We take immense trouble to select only the most readable books and therefore many people collect the entire series.

Extracts from each and every one of our books can be read on our website, at www.travelbooks.co.uk. If you would like a free copy of our catalogue, please order it from the website, email us or send a postcard.